D0726133

Joe Smith is Lecturer in Environment in the Social Sciences Faculty at the Open University. All of his work seeks to promote understanding of – and action on – global environmental issues. He teaches on environmental politics at both undergraduate and Master's levels. Two current research projects address the politics of sustainable consumption and the role of the media in shaping public debate of environment and development issues. He has worked as consultant on a range of environment-related TV programmes on BBC1, BBC2 and BBC4. Joe is also centrally involved in communications projects aimed at promoting public understanding and debate of complex environment and development issues. He is Co-Director of the Cambridge Media and Environment Programme, a series of seminars that bring together senior media decision-makers and leading specialists to consider the obstacles to effective media coverage of these issues. He is also initiator and chair of the Interdependence Day project, a research and communications initiative aimed at taking forward debates about environmental change and globalization issues. Interdependence Day includes public events and popular publications; academic research and seminars and also aims to promote new partnerships that will open up more cultural space around environmental change and globalization.

Images of ocean life were plentiful in the 1970s. These can seem clichéd now; but whales and dolphins – famed for their intelligence and skill – were cast by the Greens as photogenic creatures threatened by destructive human behaviour.

SERIES EDITOR: TONY MORRIS

Available now

What Do Buddhists Believe? Tony Morris
What Do Druids Believe? Philip Carr-Gomm
What Do Muslims Believe? Ziauddin Sardar
What Do Astrologers Believe? Nicholas Campion
What Do Existentialists Believe? Richard Appignanesi
What Do Christians Believe? Malcolm Guite
What Do Jews Believe? Edward Kessler

Forthcoming

What Do Hindus Believe? Rachel Dwyer
What Do Pagans Believe? Graham Harvey
What Do Zionists Believe? Colin Schindler

What Do
GREENS
Believe?

Joe Smith

Granta Books
London

Granta Publications, 2/3 Hanover Yard, Noel Road, London N1 8BE
First published in Great Britain by Granta Books 2006

Copyright © Joe Smith 2006

Joe Smith has asserted his moral right under the
Copyright, Designs and Patents Act, 1988, to be
identified as the author of this work.

All rights reserved. No reproduction, copy or transmissions
of this publication may be made without written
permission. No paragraph of this publication may be
reproduced, copied or transmitted save with written
permission or in accordance with the provisions of the
Copyright Act 1956 (as amended). Any person who does
any unauthorized act in relation to this publication may be
liable to criminal prosecution and civil claims for damages.

A CIP catalogue record for this book is available
from the British Library.

ISBN-13: 978-1-86207-860-4
ISBN-10: 1-86207-860-2

1 3 5 7 9 10 8 6 4 2

Typeset by M Rules
Printed and bound in Great Britain by
Bookmarque Ltd, Croydon, Surrey

For my parents, Nick and Gretchen Smith

Contents

Acknowledgements

Thanks to Andy Dobson, Liza Griffin, Roger Harrabin, Petr Jehlicka, Stephen Peake, Matt Prescott, Renata Tyszczuk and Kathryn Yusoff, who offered very helpful comments on the text or in discussion on this and related work. This book was one of a number of things started during a very fulfilling Visiting Fellowship at Clare Hall, Cambridge, in 2004. I must also thank Tony Morris for his patient and careful editorial guidance delivered in the most warm and thoughtful manner and Granta's George Miller, Sajidah Ahmad and Bella Shand for additional advice and help.

Acknowledgement

Introduction

The world's first elected Green Party members of parliament entered the West German Bundestag in 1983. They were all wearing brightly coloured clothes and carrying potted plants. The visual message was simple: a new way of doing politics had arrived, with life, not economic growth, at its centre. This was a graphic illustration of the green movement's determination to bring ecology into politics. Their actions felt novel at the time, but in fact their statement sat within a longer history of efforts to change the way the world works. Over more than a century many different modes of expression and styles of politics have been recruited to the environmental cause, from poetry to pamphleteering and from electoral politics to direct action.

In this book I am going to sketch the origins of the green movement, take a brisk tour of some of its key thinkers and ideas and explore some of the ways greens propose to 'save the world'.[1] Along the way I want to raise difficult questions for this influential movement.

The greens can at first seem a puzzle. They are a distinctive and important social movement, but difficult to pin down. They are too diverse to be said to have a clear ideology or a coherent political philosophy, and have enjoyed only relatively modest political success. Yet they are generating powerful ideas that promise to be vital to human societies as they negotiate the challenges of the twenty-first century.

The green movement has sought to transform the way we think about our relationship with the natural world and with future generations. While there is a spectrum of positions within it, from radical to reformist, the green movement has always shared a sense of urgency regarding the waste, suffering and hazards that result from our current relationship with our environment. They want us to redefine the nature of work, rethink the nature of political decision-making and overturn long-established orthodoxies in business and economics. This, they argue, is needed if we are to stave off imminent ecological catastrophe. But the ambition of the movement can look faintly comic when compared with its modest size and political weight. One of the key questions I will ask is: do the greens have the capacity to provoke the changes that are needed?

This book generally refers to 'the greens' or the green movement as its subject. The people I've lumped together may not always identify themselves as such; greens have also been referred to at different times and in different contexts as environmentalists, conservationists, political ecologists and a few others besides. The variety of these terms reflects the fact that the changing relationship between human societies and their environments has generated many different responses. When I refer to greens and the green movement, however, I am, for the sake of efficiency, drawing together the whole spectrum, from small groups of radical ecological activists to political green parties to environmental groups who work with business and government, armchair environmentalists and all positions in between. I will analyse these separately at relevant moments.

But this book tries to stand back to give a sense of the whole canvas over which the movement is spread. It aims to illuminate some of the key contributions it can make in terms of addressing some of the world's most urgent problems.

1

Who are the greens?

It is easy to think of environmental politics as something new, born of the present. Emerging as a social movement in the early 1970s and a political force in the 1980s, the greens could be thought of as a fresh-faced youngster on the political stage. But the green movement has a past stretching back over more than a century of philosophical musings, scientific findings, incidents of environmental damage and social and political change. To help place the movement forged by these diverse influences I am going to sketch a brief history in order to make sense of their main arguments. It will also trace the sources of the tensions that continue to hamper their ambitions.

What are the roots of environmentalism?

The green movement has no single starting point. Some historians go back to the late Middle Ages when measures were proposed for managing the water quality of the Thames and the air quality of London. Others identify the late seventeenth-century writer, John Evelyn, as a proto-green. Evelyn charted the problems of deforestation in England and air pollution in London. However, given that it is the link between economic development and environmental degradation that drives so much of green thinking today, it makes sense to go back just two hundred years to the Industrial Revolution.

For most of their history the greens have been an almost inaudible minority of opposition to the onward march of economic development. Yet the Industrial Revolution, and the rapid urbanization and growth of consumerism that went with it, catalysed artistic, philosophical and political reactions that still echo through current debates. The practical effects of early green thinking took time to become felt, but when we bite into a rare variety of organic apple, walk in a national park (or, more frequently, look at a photo of one), we are experiencing their influence.

Industry, trade, urbanization and mass consumption all dramatically transformed the landscape of nineteenth-century Europe. The Romantic movement in the arts and literature evolved in part as a reaction to this: poets such as Coleridge and Wordsworth viewed nature as a vital repository of beauty, spiritual renewal and fulfilment and were convinced of its potential to transform human experience.

The impulses that inspired their poetry also emerged in new ways of looking at politics. This is clearest in the writings of William Morris (1834–96), a figure best known as a designer. His debt to Romanticism is clear in his statement that 'the pleasure that resides in art is identical with that which dwells in nature'. But the view from his window was not a picturesque English rural landscape: he looked out on the world's first megalopolis – the sprawling and polluted vastness of late nineteenth-century London. Morris found it a 'sordid and loathsome place'.[2] He was repelled by contemporary culture and argued that the 'poison of riches' was leaching beauty out of the land. He warned that '(g)reen and beautiful places are still left in the countryside of England but the hand of decay is on them'.

For a time Morris was supportive of the efforts of the newly formed conservation bodies, such as the Commons Preservation Society which sought to protect open spaces to allow for appreciation of their natural beauty. But as a likeminded contemporary, Robert Somervell, put it, these scattered instances of preservation, of 'occasional and hurried glimpses of strange beauty' were woefully inadequate.[3] At the same time as arguing that all art should be based in nature Morris also came to conclude that the future of art rested with the working classes. For this to happen the conditions and purposes of labour would have to be transformed. He therefore carried the Romantic impulse into the fields of political and social commentary.

Morris's vision of a utopian society, presented in *News from Nowhere*, is of a community of contented craftworkers liberated from industrial capitalism, social structures and money. Old Hammond, one of the central characters, is, in contrast with contemporary Victorian workers, 'free, happy and energetic'. In the book Morris bound together ethics, aesthetics, his perspective towards nature, and socialist thinking about the evils of the capitalist system.[4] This is a blend that can be found in a lot of present-day green political thinking. But it offers a challenging legacy for the twenty-first century. For this early green thinker was not proposing modest stepwise reforms of the existing system. Rather, he wrote in the starkest terms about the need for its total transformation, and the dismal destination of the current trajectory of politics and economics:

Apart from the desire to produce beautiful things, the leading passion of my life has been and is hatred of modern civilization . . . Think of it. Was it all to end in a counting house on top of a cinder heap, with . . . a Whig committee dealing out champagne to the rich and margarine to the poor in such convenient proportions as would make all men contented together, though the pleasure of the eyes was gone from the world?[5]

In parallel with Morris's utopian and radical thinking, more pragmatic campaigners were creating what became major environmentalist and conservationist institutions. For example, Britain's Royal Society for the Protection of Birds,[6] one of the longest established environmental lobby organizations, began at this time, as did the National Trust. In the USA and elsewhere the movement for national parks was gaining ground and the conservationist Sierra Club was founded. Then as now, the rhetoric of green radicalism stood in stark contrast with the gently paced reformism of the conservation bodies.

The green movement has always had contradictions stitched into the fabric of its history: radicalism versus reform; preservationism alongside an impulse for revolutionary change; romantic visions imbued with an imagined past next to a desire for bold social experiment. The perplexing mix we see in the Victorian early environmentalists remains to this day.

In nineteenth-century North America there existed a similar concern about the fast-growing cities, and the impact of society on the natural world. But early American environmentalists were primarily concerned at the heavy footprint of expanding human activity in what they viewed as a vast wilderness. The early American conservationist/preservationist movement pointed to the rapid loss of what were seen as pristine, 'empty' wild places (of course Native Americans didn't think of them as wild or empty at all). One of the founding figures of this movement, the writer Ralph Waldo Emerson, had travelled in Europe and met the English Romantic poets. In 1836 he published *Nature*, a homily to the unity of nature, science and spirituality. In Emerson's philosophy/religion of Transcendentalism, nature offered evidence of the presence of the divine in all things.

Emerson's acolyte, Henry David Thoreau, took this philosophy so seriously that he embarked on a two-year experiment, living on nature and his wits, next to Walden pond, Maine. He opens his now celebrated book, *Walden*, with the statement: 'When I wrote the following pages . . . I lived alone, in the woods, a mile from any neighbor, in a house which I had built myself . . . and earned my living by the labor of my own hands only.'[7] A few pages later he exhorts the increasingly wealthy American society to 'simplify, simplify', and demonstrates in his account of his experiment how humans can live harmoniously with nature. Explaining his decision to embark on the experiment he wrote that:

> I went to the woods because I wished to live deliberately, to front only the essential facts of life, and see if I could not learn what it had to teach, and not, when I came to die, discover that I had not lived. I did not wish to live what was not life, living is so dear; nor did I wish to practice resignation, unless it was quite necessary. I wanted to live deep and suck out all the marrow of life, to live so sturdily and Spartan-like as to put to rout all that was not life.[8]

His self-published volume sold almost no copies at the time (he once joked that his library contained thousands of books, most of which he had written himself). But this quest for an authentic life in nature became essential reading for modern American environmentalists and is in print in numerous editions today.

Thoreau is celebrated by greens for his promotion of civil disobedience, his critique of industrialized labour and his romantic evocation of a life lived in harmony with the natural world. His sturdy virtues of individualism, self-sufficiency and honest hard work, alongside his belief in the spiritual benefits of preserving natural wilderness, fit comfortably with several of the United States' founding myths. Indeed his mentor Emerson suggested that 'no truer American exists than Thoreau'. This vision has nourished North American greens as they have sought to argue for alternatives to unqualified and inexorable economic growth.

Thoreau argued for national policies to protect 'wilderness' after seeing the devastation logging wrought on the once expansive Maine forest. In due course a small but influential lobby for national parks and nature conservation developed and by 1916 a national park service was established. It is a mistake, however, to caricature American conservationists as only concerned with the preservation of these places for their own sake. Some of the major conservationist figures of the first half of the twentieth century, such as the hiker Robert Marshall, co-founder of the Wilderness Society, saw the sustenance of wild places as essential to the public health of urban populations. Photographer Ansel Adams's images did much to communicate a sense of awe and wonder at the USA's (apparent) wilderness. Protecting the parks was also seen as a way of soothing the ills of twentieth-century urban America.

American environmentalists led the way in constructing a view of pristine nature which proved to be important in 'building a movement', and remains so today. Adams's sublime images and the art and writing of the Romantic movement have helped to build up a rich stock of cultural references. But there are dangers in projecting 'fragile nature' as something that starts where the tarmac runs out. The stark split between cities and wilderness in American pre-war environmentalists' writings and Adams's photographs have led environmentalism to neglect cities as an environment. These are the places where most people in the world now live – and are part of nature too. In this way the green movement may have done more to sustain a damaging split between nature and culture than to abolish it. Quite apart from being an incomplete (and none too ecological) view of the world, it could be argued that this has made it *more* not less difficult for them to build stronger and broader alliances.

Economic boom and environmental bust

If the first great flowering of environmentalist thought and action grew as a response to the burst of economic development in the late nineteenth century, the second arose as a direct consequence of the economic boom which occurred after the Second World War. Specific pollution events and new scientific findings helped to create a modern environmental consciousness.

London – the world's first mega-city – provided perhaps the most notorious example. It had been known for the dismal quality of its air and water for centuries. However the smogs (a dense and choking mix of smoke and fog) of 1952 were of an altogether different order. The rapidly growing use of petrol engines, plus the burning of domestic and industrial solid fuel, combined with the weather to produce dangerously low air quality. At their peak the smogs are thought to have caused the death of more than four thousand people in London in a single year. Public reaction led to legislative change – and rapid improvements in air quality – in the years that followed.

Such events suggested that modern life, for all its new products and conveniences, carried new risks. This was further underlined by another pollution event on the other side of the world. In 1956 a small Japanese fishing port gave its name to a mysterious disease that has, to the present day, affected more than three thousand people in two areas of Japan. Research revealed industrial mercury leaking into fisheries as the cause. The Chisso corporation, which initially denied releasing mercury compounds into Minamata Bay, was eventually forced to accept blame for the health-threatening industrial pollution. And only after decades of evasion did they pay compensation to more than three thousand officially recognized victims.

The surprise success of a book on the impact of the chemical pesticide DDT in the USA suggested that society was increasingly ready to hear difficult news about the downsides to economic growth. Scientist Rachel Carson's *Silent Spring*, published in 1962, argued that this wonder chemical, which had served in the fight against typhus and malaria, brought with it devastating long-term consequences. The book sought to show that its indiscriminate use was transforming the natural world in calamitous ways. It seems an improbable best-seller. But Carson, like many of the environmentalists who followed her, was a great storyteller with a strong instinct for emotive phrases: the title of the book derived from the suggestion that DDT would kill off songbirds. The threat of a silent spring captured the public imagination, as did her account of how persistent chemicals released in America's industrial heartlands could find their way into the body tissue of Antarctic penguins. She proposed biological controls on unwanted insects as an alternative. In this way a single popular science writer showed it was possible to force the immensely powerful chemical industry onto the defensive when they mounted an extensive public relations campaign against her arguments.

It is no coincidence that these three separate episodes in modern environmentalism came about in three of the power-houses of post-war economic development: Britain, Japan and the USA. They were not the only significant events in the story between 1945 and the early 1960s. But they did show some of the main features of environmental conflict in the last decades of the twentieth century.

These cases pre-dated the organized environmental campaigning of the 1970s and 1980s, and did not mobilize mass protest. But they did show that a combination of expert witnesses, evidence of victims (whether human or not) and media interest could combine powerfully. The UK government, the Japanese chemical industry and American agribusiness were all forced onto the defensive, and ultimately changed their policies and practices in response to environmental scandals. These incidents gave impetus to arguments about governmental and corporate environmental responsibility. They also showed the role of the modern news media in the promotion of public understanding and the growth of environmental consciousness. Environmental disaster stories made good copy and provided lurid images for news media that increasingly sought sensation, drama and novelty.

The London smogs, Minamata disease and the success of *Silent Spring* contributed to a growing public awareness of human impacts on the environment. The idea that environmental responsibility stretched far beyond local and national boundaries began to lodge. Environmentalists insisted that the wealth of the developed world had been won at a cost to the natural world and to human health. Human survival, environmentalists now argued, would depend on breaking this cycle of economic growth and environmental destruction.

The late 1960s and early 1970s saw modern environmentalism emerge, in parallel with the women's and the peace movements, as a new kind of social movement. The Apollo moon landings provided an immensely powerful visual badge in the form of the 'blue marble' image of the planet from space. This view of what was often described at the time as a fragile earth chimed neatly with the environmentalist motto: 'Think global, act local'.

The Secretary-General of the United Nations, U Thant, summed up the mood of the moment in his Earth Day Proclamation, 1971, on a day of globally observed events intended to inspire change:

A new world view is emerging. Through the eyes of our astronauts and cosmonauts we now see our beautiful blue planet as a home for all people . . . Planet Earth is facing a grave crisis which only the people of Earth can resolve, and the delicate balances of nature, essential for our survival, can only be saved through a global effort, involving all of us.[9]

Millions of people participated in rallies and other events on the first Earth Day in 1970, and the first United Nations Conference on the Human Environment was held in Stockholm in 1972. A new way of looking at humanity's place in the world was emerging.

Particular kinds of images were important in symbolizing and reinforcing this new perspective. Nowhere is this better illustrated than in the media coverage and public reaction to the world's first serious oil tanker disaster off the south coast of Britain in March 1967. The *Torrey Canyon* hit rocks, and its leaked fuel found its way onto British and French beaches. Although the size of the tanker and the amount of leaked oil was modest by today's standards, the public was gripped by its fate. Prime Minister Harold Wilson eventually sent RAF planes to bomb the ship in the hope of igniting the remaining oil. This visually arresting but largely meaningless action was in itself a measure of the changing significance of environmental issues for both mainstream politicians and the media.

Oil was central to another important event: the so-called oil crisis of 1973. This was not an environmental event per se: oil-producing countries of the Middle East were successful in restricting the supply of a natural resource that was by now the lifeblood of developed-world economies. But the event illustrated what environmentalist writers had been predicting about the consequences of resource scarcity. The fourfold increases in crude oil prices bolstered environmentalist arguments that linked industrial development, resource exploitation and the crisis.

In 1976 at Seveso in Italy an infamous chemical accident occurred, which resulted in the release of a dense vapour cloud of dioxins from a plant producing herbicides and pesticides. Two thousand people were treated for poisoning, more than six hundred evacuated from their homes and ten square miles of land were contaminated. In 1978 the tanker *Amoco Cadiz* ran aground off the north-west coast of France spilling 68.7 million gallons of oil. At the end of the decade the world's first major non-military nuclear disaster occurred at the Three Mile Island plant in Pennsylvania, when one of the two reactors suffered a meltdown. Local and national uncertainty amongst politicians and officials about the hazards to the population and environment undermined confidence in an industry that demanded high levels of capital investment and political support.

These are only a few of the events that engaged and fed the public's concern and moulded modern environmentalism. The oil, chemical and nuclear industries were identified as the prime targets. Agriculture and forestry soon joined the list as research emerged to show the increasing prevalence of hazardous levels of soil erosion, desertification and loss of biological diversity. The growing catalogue of environmental woes both contributed to, and was a reflection of, the growth of popular concern. And it all fed an increasingly influential green movement.

New forms of organization and new ways of doing politics were emerging in many spheres of life. The women's movement and the peace movement, like the environmental movement, were aiming not solely to influence policy and political argument, but also to change the underlying culture. For these new social movements personal was becoming inseparable from political life. But this internalizing of politics did not get in the way of the formation of new campaigning institutions. Friends of the Earth was founded in the USA in 1969, and Greenpeace in 1971 in Canada.

Both organizations blended the personal and the political with a distinctive new style of campaigning. From the start they used direct action alongside clever deployment of research findings and strong images to win media space, excite public sympathy and provoke a response from the political and business communities. Other long-established environmental groups such as the Sierra Club in the USA and the Royal

Society for the Protection of Birds in the UK benefited from the growing prominence of the more radical new groups. As 'environmentalists you could do business with' the authority of the older groups was enhanced in government and business circles. A spectrum of campaigning methods began to develop, which has long been seen as one of the green movement's greatest strengths. It contributed to a number of major breakthroughs in local, national and international environmental legislation.

Most accounts of the green movement suggest that environmentalism is a trend found only in rich societies, as if there is an evolution towards the emergence of environmentalist values. Commentators have tended to neglect the growth of environmental protest in the developing world, particularly concerning mining, dam projects and deforestation. The Chipko Movement, born in 1973 in India, and the Green Belt Movement, started in Kenya in 1977, are prime examples. These applied different methods of environmental protest: non-violent direct action. The protests carried out by the Chipko Movement were highly effective. Villagers (mostly women) hugged trees that were threatened by loggers, and used the attention these actions gained to explain how the trees were an essential part of their daily lives. Similarly the Green Belt Movement's community tree planting captured the local and international imagination. This inspiring work resulted many years later in a Nobel Peace Prize for its founder, Wangari Maathai.

Environmentalism in the developing world is not a copycat of its developed-world cousin, but represents a different kind of work and thought. Some of the principles and practices have migrated from south to north; this fact is nicely summarized in the fact that it was Gandhi who coined the environmentalist epigram: 'The world has enough for everybody's need, but not enough for one person's greed.'

GANDHI'S IDEAL VILLAGE

It will have cottages with sufficient light and ventilation,
built of a material obtainable within a radius of five miles of
it. The cottages will have courtyards enabling householders
to plant vegetables for domestic use and to house their
cattle . . . It will have houses of worship for all, also a
common meeting place, a village common for grazing its
cattle, a co-operative dairy, primary and secondary schools
in which industrial [i.e. vocational] education will be the
central fact, and it will have Panchayats [village councils]
for settling disputes. It will produce its own grains,
vegetables and fruit, and its own Khadi [hand-spun cotton].
This is roughly my idea of a model village . . .[10]

The Gandhian tradition of non-violent direct action that the
Green Belt and Chipko movements, amongst others, practised
so effectively have become central tools for developed-world
environmentalists. Similarly, the Chilean economist, Manfred
Max-Neef, who coined the term 'barefoot economics', added
plausibility to some theoretical arguments. He showed first-
hand examples of how green economics could work on the
ground in developing countries. These movements' concern
with social justice as the root cause of environmental
danger also began to feed into the thinking of developed-
world environmentalists. In the USA this took the form of
the environmental justice movement. Shocking events such as
the Bhopal chemical disaster in India in 1984, when poisonous
clouds of gas affected thousands of people, and the scandal
surrounding the murder by ranchers of Chico Mendes, leader

of the Chiapas rubber tappers' union in 1988, soldered the connection.[11]

What were environmentalists reading?

Intellectual debate and political action were tightly bound together in the development of the green movement in the early 1970s. Paul Ehrlich's *The Population Bomb* linked growth in human population, resource exploitation and environmental degradation in a simple formula that continues to play in the background of much environmentalist debate. Following similar lines, the Club of Rome, a group of senior industrialists and academics, published its controversial and influential *Limits to Growth* report in 1972. With the aid of computer modelling, the report identified unfettered economic growth as the central culprit in environmental devastation.

In 1973, the economist, Fritz Schumacher, joined the debate with a book that remains a classic. The green movement is short on leaders and ideology – that's how it likes it – but Schumacher is high on any greens' list of influential thinkers. *Small Is Beautiful* dismissed some of the central tenets of mainstream economic thinking with all the cheeky imposture of the boy observing that the emperor has no clothes on:

> One of the most fateful errors of our age is the belief that 'the problem of production' has been solved . . . A businessman would not consider a firm to have solved its problems of production and to have achieved viability if he saw that it was rapidly consuming its capital. How, then, could we overlook this vital fact when it comes to that very big firm, the economy

of Spaceship Earth and, in particular, the economies of its rich passengers?[12]

Schumacher was better qualified than most to criticize economics on this scale: he was a respected expert who had spent decades with the UK's National Coal Board. Two of his central concerns were scale and appropriateness. He wanted to show the waste and inhumanity that were the inevitable result of ever more centralized and unwieldy economic units; he stressed that these units could only be broken down to a more human scale if technology were itself made more humane and *appropriate*. There is a strong echo of Gandhi's work here, as elsewhere in modern environmentalist thought. In place of mass production, Schumacher proposed production by the masses. This would, he argued, be more 'conducive to decentralisation, compatible with the laws of ecology, gentle in its use of scarce resources, and designed to serve the human person instead of making him the servant of machines'.[13] His was a vision of 'intermediate' or appropriate technology, accessible and controllable by the poorest citizens in the world (but also relevant to the richest). It would be designed to meet people's essential needs without threatening the environment. The focus on a revision of what human societies and economies meant by the word 'need' was strongly influenced by his contact with Buddhist scholars.

Schumacher believed that any debate about economics and environment should refer back to the clear physical laws that were understood and obeyed in so many other areas in life. In this way he was, like the other best-selling environmental authors of his day, splicing scientific knowledge and physical laws together with ethical calls to action on waste and suffering in the world. The time was right: their work was hitting the bookshelves at a time when environmental disasters were major media events, and the work of these green writers raced to prominence in mainstream media and political debate.

In the same year as *Limits to Growth* was published, the first major international environmental conference was held in Stockholm. The UN Conference on the Human Environment (UNCHE) was in some ways a dress rehearsal for the two decades of environmental politics that were to follow. Environmentalists castigated businesses and governments and demanded a rethink of the way developed economies worked. They also argued that the Western model of development must not be pursued in the developing world.

There is little evidence that the first argument altered the 'business as usual' patterns of business and politics. Perhaps, more seriously, the second argument was characterized as a colonial imposition of a developed world model upon the developing world. Developing-world leaders promptly set themselves in firm opposition. The report, *Only One Earth* (1972), linked to the UNCHE, concluded that a shared concern for the planet's future, in a spirit of common stewardship rather than dominion, was the only way forward. But in reality the core of environmentalist thinking at this time was deeply divisive. It offered an untried, unpalatable and hazardous route for mainstream politics and business in the developed world and appeared to deny the developing world the benefits of progress that Western environmentalists had already enjoyed.

The tide turned against green thinking in the late 1970s. Despite the doom-laden and urgent prophecies of scarcity and disaster, the developed world survived two oil-price crises – and the computer-generated projections of population and resource catastrophes did not come about. It was to be more than a decade before green thinking could again win a sympathetic and widespread hearing.

If the 1970s was a decade of innovation and growth, the early 1980s saw the environmentalist movement enter a period of consolidation and institutionalization. Disasters such as the Bhopal leakage of toxic gases in India in 1984, which killed 10,000 over time, and the Chernobyl nuclear reactor explosion in Ukraine in 1986 fuelled the fast-growing membership of environmental organizations. Greenpeace and Friends of the Earth matured into sophisticated campaigning agencies that pursued carefully targeted goals at national and international levels. They were focused on industrial pollution and the protection of species and habitats, or biodiversity, as it came to be known. Ongoing research into biodiversity loss gave scientific legitimacy and impetus to the green case.

Biologists in the mid-1980s confirmed that the diversity found in the living world appeared to be shrinking fast as a consequence of human development. They coined the term 'biodiversity' to summarize the diversity of life on earth, and to help to focus research and policy effort. Environmentalists have deployed emotive icons of species loss since the late 1960s, above all large mammals such as whales, tigers and pandas as emblems of the threatened global environment. The first hard evidence of loss of diversity came with assessments of tropical deforestation. These were the most concentrated areas of biodiversity on the planet, and scientists found disturbingly rapid rates of loss. These findings have been repeated in other habitats around the world, from oceans to deserts. This research was part of a potent mix that combined with the green movement's increasingly skilful campaigning to put pressure on politicians to act.

Although this has led to statements of concern it hasn't led to anything more than sporadic policy action. For all its successes the green movement in the 1980s failed to engage with the fast-moving economic and political debates of the time. They had no response to match the compelling energy and scale of economic globalization. The most they offered was a blunt opposition to globalization and corporations. Despite insisting on the urgency of the ecological crisis they have generally failed to convince the media and public that they offer plausible alternatives.

The greens seem to have found it difficult to answer the hard questions about economic development. Environmental and resource economists, ecologists and demographers equipped the green movement with some powerful tools. But the 1970s literature also left the greens with an under-explored and deep-set opposition to economic development. This left them excluded from political debate in the fast-changing circumstances of the following decades.

Their reluctance to develop common cause with other potentially supportive constituencies, above all, in the 1970s and 1980s, with social democrat parties of the centre and left, or anti-poverty movements, left the green case underdeveloped. The 'reformist' wing of the movement had little to say about the workings of the increasingly global structure of corporations who organized themselves very effectively across vast distributed networks. One of the lessons of the early 1970s that the movement forgot was that they can provoke improbable but powerful alliances, such as the Club of Rome's mix of senior business, political and academic figures. Such alliances can carry ideas much further than the isolated fundamentalism that many greens condemned themselves to in the years that followed.

Greens have also tended to translate the works of Schumacher and other environmental economists as favouring an uncomplicated localism. For this reason the green movement has until recently had little impact on the course of debates about the post-cold war world and globalization. The late 1980s and early 1990s was a period of enormous opportunity, which invited new ways of thinking about the relationship between states, markets and nature. Technological advances allowed fast, cheap and well-focused networks to develop. But the green movement failed to capture the moment. Here is a paradox: despite being perhaps the first genuinely 'global' movement, the greens did not organize themselves effectively on an international level at a time when corporations were doing precisely that.

Moving towards the first global politics

Despite piecemeal advances in the development of environmental legislation across the developed world, the political tide was flowing strongly against green ideas. Indeed, leaders such as Margaret Thatcher and Ronald Reagan sought to accelerate economic development in the opposite direction. Neo-liberal strategies for responding to economic globalization, increasingly dominant across the developed world in the 1980s and 1990s, set out to offer the best conditions for rapid economic development. Environmental protection was seen as an obstacle in an increasingly competitive global marketplace.

It may be that this deeply unpromising context itself helped to generate an important political innovation within the environmental movement: the emergence of new political parties, explicitly founded upon ecological principles. Green parties wanted to take environmentalists' critiques of the modern world directly into the domain of mainstream politics.

This was in part because people started to understand environmental issues in new ways in the 1980s. Much environmental regulation had occurred around pollution hotspots, where local culprits were easily identified. Over time, the transnational nature of much pollution became an increasingly important aspect of environmental politics. Recognition of the fact that pollution does not respect frontiers lent further weight to the new environmental politics. Analysis of water pollution, for example on the Rhine and Danube rivers in Europe and the Great Lakes in North America, demonstrated that multilateral agreements among affected parties were essential. Collaborative work by environmentalists from all the countries affected by or causing pollution in the Rhine region demonstrated that environmental problems are transnational. It also proved that green politics could be too.

In the early 1980s the public first became aware of the issue of acid rain, or acidification, a topic which Swedish scientists had begun working on in the late 1960s. In the decade that followed evidence piled up that 'forest die-back' in parts of Germany, Scandinavia and Canada was being caused by airborne sulphur pollution. The term 'acid rain', or acid deposition, describes how sulphur oxides originating from industrial sources such as coal-fired power stations or metal smelters can affect ecosystems hundreds of miles away. Although acid rain is associated in the public mind with damage to coniferous forests, the first effects are felt in surface waters where the process threatens acid-sensitive organisms including fish, many amphibians, snails and so on. Acid rain also erodes metals, limestone and marble. Some of the world's most famous monuments, such as Trajan's column in Rome and the Parthenon in Greece, suffered more rapid erosion in the space of two decades than they had in preceding centuries. Whether it was dying forests or crumbling buildings, the green movement's growth was nourished by such culturally powerful threats.

Research began to map the most likely sources. Lengthy debates and difficult negotiations began within the European Community and made clear how protracted and difficult international environmental politics can be. West Germany (driven in large part by its increasingly influential green movement and environmental public awareness) pressed for greatly reduced sulphur emissions. British politicians and scientists contested German and Scandinavian interpretations of the evidence that suggested that emissions from the burning of high sulphur-content coal in Britain were being blown across Europe and deposited on Scandinavian and German forests. They argued that proposed regulations to clean up European industry, and in particular coal-powered electricity generating plants, would be economically damaging. Once agreements were eventually reached, acid rain levels were reduced relatively quickly. This showed that environmentalist pressure and mounting scientific consensus could deliver change even in the context of difficult international agreements.

Developed-world environmentalists had not forgotten their concern with the impact of rapid economic development on the environment in the developing world. Poorer countries were facing the 'first generation' environmental problems of air, water and soil pollution caused by industrialization. But rapid changes in land use were also accelerating the loss of biodiversity. At the same time, economic development in poorer countries had faltered and global financial institutions were becoming increasingly influential in decision-making in the developing world. In 1983 the UN Secretary-General convened a high-level World Commission on Environment and Development (WCED), in an attempt to identify ways to achieve both the economic development and environmental protection that had eluded all parties since the Stockholm conference of 1972.

The Norwegian premier, Gro Harlem Brundtland, took the chair and guided the drafting of its findings. The 'Brundtland Report' was published in 1987 as *Our Common Future*: the main outcome of its exhaustive analysis of the environment and development debates of the time was the promotion of the concept of sustainable development. This concept had been present in environmentalist debates for some years but the WCED now promoted it as central to global economic development. The report was drafted with great political and diplomatic skill. Environmentalists could see their concerns expressed in it. At the same time the pursuit of economic development in the developing world was supported. All this was achieved in the politically deft 'Brundtland definition' of 'a form of sustainable development which meets the needs of the present without compromising the ability of future generations to meet their own needs'.

Drawing together threads of environmentalist thinking from the previous two decades, the report identified some key problems. The lack of effective environmental protection institutions and information, especially in the developing world, was foremost. Added to this was the absence of integration across agencies working on environment and development. The report also pressed for much closer working between government, business and NGOs. The Brundtland report also demanded more comprehensive and effective environmental agreements. Despite the careful wording and breadth of support for its general principles, it did not propel global leaders to action. Instead its subtle political manoeuvring served to build a promise that environmental protection and economic development could be achieved – the circle could be squared. This provided environment ministers with a comforting rhetorical device. It also created some new terrain from which greens could embark on terminological warfare with mainstream politicians. But the practical effects were almost imperceptible. It took the emergence into political consciousness of new kinds of global environmental threat at the very end of the 1980s to catalyse the next phase in the development of environmental politics.

Environmentalists had portrayed themselves as a global movement since late 1960s. Ever since the Apollo mission beamed back the 'blue marble' photograph of earth from space, environmentalists had adopted this iconic image to reflect their concern with what they viewed as a fragile and interconnected whole. But the issues in which they were engaged could only be considered global in the sense that pollution and loss of species and habitats did not stop at national boundaries. It was concern with the ozone layer that finally prompted a new way of thinking about global human-environment interactions. In 1985 a team of scientists working in Antarctica found a thinning of up to 50% of the ozone layer above the pole. This was dubbed the 'ozone hole', and was found to be caused by a family of industrially produced chemicals known as chlorofluorocarbons (CFCs). CFCs had been widely used in refrigeration, cleaning and packaging products, and as gas propellants since the 1950s; now they were implicated in the destruction of a layer of gas that protected the earth from harmful levels of ultraviolet radiation.

THE 'OZONE HOLE'

Between ten and fifty miles above the earth a layer of ozone gas serves to prevent 99% of the sun's ultraviolet-B radiation from reaching the planet's surface. Scientific research has shown that in the last few decades the chemistry of this previously stable layer has been disrupted by the presence of CFCs. It has been found that in the presence of the ultraviolet radiation in the stratosphere, CFCs decompose and release chlorine. This chlorine molecule in turn reacts with ozone, resulting in an oxygen molecule and chlorine monoxide. This sets up a chain reaction, in which one chlorine molecule can destroy thousands of ozone molecules. Because of their stability, CFCs cause problems in the stratosphere for a century or more. Although ozone depletion is not confined to the poles, the thinning of the ozone layer has been particularly evident there because of the nature of the polar winters. The discovery of the ozone hole represented a startling new turn in environmental understanding. Scientific evidence demanded that society recognize that a myriad of individual choices about the design and use of everyday products was altering the global environment. Environmental groups were central to the process of lodging the issue in the public mind.

This 'hole' could be shown in clear, irrefutable maps. The science was solid and the causes well understood. This helped to make the threat to both human and planetary health real and therefore it generated rapid media, public and political concern.

In 1987 the Montreal Protocol was signed resulting in agreement around the progressive phasing out of CFCs and associated ozone-depleting chemicals. Decades have still to pass before existing CFCs cease to deplete the ozone layer. Also, CFC allowances for developing countries together with a substantial black market in CFCs will further delay that repair. But the Montreal Protocol does represent an important precedent as an international environmental agreement. Left to scientists and diplomats alone it is impossible to imagine that action would have been so swift; the green movement helped to translate scientific knowledge into public concern and in turn political pressure.

The same entrepreneurial and creative resources were applied to an issue that has proved to have far greater reach and significance: climate change. In their research on climate change (often described as global warming), the scientific community were uncovering an immense challenge to society. It was to lend a new authority and legitimacy to the green movement and the concept of sustainable development in the early 1990s.

Since the early nineteenth century there had been theories about how a 'blanket' of carbon dioxide [CO_2] surrounding the earth might serve to maintain higher temperatures on earth than would otherwise be the case. The French scientist, Fourier, had first suggested there might be a 'greenhouse effect' in 1827. At the end of the century the Swedish scientist, Arrhenius, proposed that the growing volume of CO_2 emitted since the Industrial Revolution was changing the composition of the atmosphere. He suggested that this would enhance the greenhouse effect, thereby causing the earth's temperature to rise.

The starting point for the modern science of climate change was the International Geophysical Year in 1957. This established a global community of researchers concerned with planetary processes. In the years that followed, research conducted at, among other places, MIT in the USA, charted rising CO_2 levels, and pointed to the possibility of human-induced climate change. Climate scientists in the late 1970s and early 1980s had a previously unimagined capacity for data gathering and analysis. This allowed them to explore the hypothesis that the enormous quantities of CO_2 that human societies had released into the atmosphere since the Industrial Revolution (particularly since the Second World War) might be accelerating the naturally occurring greenhouse effect. The prediction that this might result in hazardous climate change began to gain ground.

The seriousness of the hazards they identified provoked the scientific and policy community into action. The creation of the Intergovernmental Panel on Climate Change (IPCC) brought together academics from a broad range of backgrounds to review all the existing evidence for the hypothesis. The IPCC amounts to the biggest peer review in the history of science. And it needs to be: making sense of the climate system is a very ambitious goal. It has published its findings in a series of weighty Assessment Reports. The first of these appeared in 1990 and, although worded very cautiously, it argued that further human-induced emissions of climate-changing gases would result in a rise in global surface temperatures with potentially damaging consequences for humans and their natural environment. Subsequent reports have been increasingly confident that we face a human-caused problem.

Climate change is the greatest recruiting sergeant that the greens have ever had, and it has moved to the centre of the work of most environmentalist organizations. Does the fact that the issue was barely on their radar until the late 1980s, but quickly became their prime concern, suggest the lack of a critical and strategic core? Their political heritage is unlike social movements of the past: there isn't a social class, professional or regional loyalty that continues to bring new people in. They need to keep on reinventing themselves if they are to have a claim on their supporters' time and money, and a legitimate claim to political and media space. The greens need to be careful to ensure that their work on climate change is part of a carefully developed long-term green strategy, and not simply a priority dictated by political opportunism.

A separate criticism of the greens in this period relates to how they fail to organize globally. Certainly the green intellectual tradition is internationalist; they believe that the causes and consequences of most major environmental problems can only be understood by looking at whole regions, continents and the weather, food, water and other systems that persist in ignorance of the historical accident of human borders. Some NGOs have also demonstrated their capacity to deploy a particularly emotive or graphically powerful event to provoke a globally coordinated response.

But surprisingly in the age of the Internet, cheap global travel and mass migration, the greens have proven to be little better in terms of coordinated international action than nineteenth-century socialists. They are certainly a long way behind the world's major companies in terms of global organization. Why did they not harness their evident capacity for creativity and energy in exposing and communicating dangers to the environment and apply it to the nature of their organization? There are few successful instances of horizontally networked global environmental action. But there are many examples of rigidly organized national bodies that are slow to agree and act with others. This failure by the greens has impeded action on the issues they have worked hard to have recognized.

Are we all greens now?

By the late 1980s and early 1990s the weight of environmental science, green campaigning and media attention came together to create an unprecedented level of pressure on politicians from all backgrounds. This moment resembled the first high tide of environmentalism in the early 1970s. There were opportunities to get major political and business players to stop and consider the radical nature of environmental problems.

The moment was marked by the largest ever gathering of world leaders at the UN Conference on Environment and Development (UNCED) in Rio de Janeiro in June 1992. The meeting, also known as the Earth Summit, sought solutions to global environmental change problems, above all climate change and biodiversity loss and placed the concept of sustainable development at its heart. The most important outcomes included a charter for sustainable development, tagged *Agenda 21*, and the drafting of UN conventions on biodiversity and climate change. These gave some structure and direction to international debate. Above all, such agreements brought environmental politics into the mainstream.

Although the green movement can claim much of the credit for the fact that UNCED came about, it had mixed reactions to the outcomes. The 'realists' and reformists felt that the commitments that had been made by politicians would allow the movement to 'ratchet forward' environmental protection. They would start to steer economic development into more environmentally sustainable forms. Some leading-edge businesses did make progress towards resource efficiency and reducing their impacts on biodiversity. Governments enhanced reporting of environmental performance, for example, through sustainable development indicators and strategies. Cross-governmental and independent bodies were set up for auditing progress.

More radical greens saw grave hazards in the stealing of environmentalist clothes by politics and business. For them 'sustainable development' was worthless and empty rhetoric. It came from the mouths of precisely those people who were overseeing policies and processes that accelerated climate change and biodiversity loss. The progress of green political parties in electoral politics was one place to take out their frustration with the empty promises of mainstream politics.

From one point of view green parties have been surprisingly successful. The first green parties were formed in 1972 in New Zealand (the Values Party) and in 1973 in the UK (the Ecology Party). The first green parliamentary breakthrough came with the German Greens winning their first parliamentary seats in 1983, barely a decade later.

Since the early 1990s green parties around the world have become increasingly experienced and professionalized, but have sought to remain true to their promise to 'bring ecology into politics'. One researcher looking at green parties' experiences in government in Europe calculated that by 2002 green parties had played a role in national government in no fewer than fifteen European countries. Collectively, 44 green government ministers (at cabinet level) had been in government for 59 years.[14]

The experience of being in elected office has demanded dealmaking and compromise. This has forced green parties to abandon some of their commitments to grassroots democracy. But these compromises have not delivered meaningful power. Central and East European greens achieved some prominence for their part in the fall of the Communist system. This led to appointments of green party ministers in some of the European post-Communist states in transition in the early 1990s. They gained footholds in government in ten countries. But they were in almost all cases overtaken by the forceful tide of economic liberalization and 'Westernization'.

The second half of the 1990s saw green parties in Western Europe experience their first sustained taste of government. Greens participated in coalition governments in Finland (1995), Italy (1996), France (1997), Germany (1998) and Belgium (1999). The most interesting and important case amongst these is Germany, where the Greens represented the sole and vital coalition partner for the SPD (Social Democratic Party) until 2005. They enjoyed mixed results, failing to win battles on energy taxation and gaining only partial victory on nuclear power. They found themselves bound into consensus on international relations – particularly questions surrounding Germany's involvement in the NATO intervention in Serbia in 1999. The German Green Party in office fell into line with the general approach of the government towards economic global-ization and liberalization. But their presence in electoral politics both inside and outside government over the last twenty years has made Germany into world leaders in terms of green policies and technologies.

Green parties have also emerged in the developing world but they are at present only a very modest force. The Brazilian Greens that formed part of President Lula da Silva's Brazilian government are one example. But the party decided to leave the government in 2005 in protest at the government's failure to implement their legislation to protect the Amazon.

Greens in government have, at best, been in weak bargaining positions, and have been forced to adapt to the political realities of short-term deal-making and incremental progress. Experience of government has demanded professionalization and political

ANTI-LEADER LEADERSHIP:
THE LIFE OF PETRA KELLY

Green parties didn't spring out of nowhere – they were made by individuals who saw an urgent need to bring ecology into politics. Born in West Germany in 1947, and educated in the United States, Petra Kelly was a co-founder of the West German Green Party (Die Grünen). She was awarded the alternative Nobel Prize – the Right Livelihood Award – in 1982 'for forging and implementing a new vision uniting ecological concerns with disarmament, social justice and human rights'. Kelly embodied the way green politics grew out of a weaving-together of the concerns of these 'citizens' movements'. She described Die Grünen as 'a non-violent ecological and basic-democratic anti-war coalition of parliamentary and extra-parliamentary grassroots-oriented forces'.

Kelly died tragically in 1992, it seems at the hands of her husband who then killed himself. Her deep commitments to non-violence and grassroots participative democracy would have been severely tested by the greens' experience of power-broking and compromise from the end of that decade. But her dynamism and political creativity summarize neatly the contribution of the movement as a whole to late twentieth-century politics. The Dalai Lama said of her: 'Petra Kelly was a committed and dedicated person with compassionate concern for the oppressed, the weak and the persecuted in our time. Her spirit and legacy of human solidarity and concern continue to inspire and encourage us all.'

sophistication. This can seem at odds with the parade of brightly dressed academics and social workers that took up Green parliamentary seats in the Bundestag in 1983. But their presence has helped to advance political debate. Where proportional representation exists their appearance, even as a minor party aiming for 5 to10% of the vote, helps to sharpen mainstream parties' attendance to ecological concerns.

Another response by green radicals to what they see as tokenistic use of green rhetoric has been to sustain the tradition of non-violent direct action. These have often been inspired by a radical environmental philosophy known as 'deep ecology'. Sometimes going under the banner of the radical organization Earth First!, they have used the most radical forms of non-violent direct action to disrupt projects and industries they see as threatening. This has usually taken the form of putting their bodies between the workers and machines of the construction, forestry and agriculture industries and the species or habitats they have sought to protect.

Campaigning environmental NGOs such as Friends of the Earth and Greenpeace have often proved to be highly effective in attracting media attention to their direct action demonstrations. Some of the best-known examples of this were the campaigns against oil companies' failures in their environmental and social responsibility. The environmental NGOs created global media platforms for particular stories that had the power to illustrate their wider case. Two examples demonstrate the potential power of this way of working: the campaign against the dumping of the Brent Spar oil storage facility in the North Sea, and that against Shell's complicity in environmental and social damage in Nigeria. In the case of Shell in Nigeria, Ken Saro-Wiwa led a campaign that saw 300,000 Ogoni men, women and children take to the streets in protest against the destruction of their homelands by the company. Soon after the protests, Nigerian military forces began attacking Ogoni villages, where thousands were killed and many more made homeless. In 1994, Saro-Wiwa was arrested, and in the following year executed. NGO campaigns in the developed world targeted the complicity of Shell in this catalogue of human rights and ecological abuses.

In the same year Shell and Greenpeace were the main actors in a media battle over the disposal of the Brent Spar oil storage platform in the North Sea. Greenpeace fought a very effective campaign to make this a test case of corporate environmental responsibility. They succeeded in winning hearts and minds and, together with the Ogoniland case, the victory was important in establishing principles of corporate social and environmental responsibility. Greenpeace suffered its own PR disaster when it admitted to making mistakes in the presentation of pollution risks. But what these instances proved was that corporate brands that had been carefully nurtured in the minds of consumers over decades were increasingly vulnerable. A new style of NGO campaigning that combined a mix of ethical appeal, scientific evidence, graphic media imagery and global surveillance could do them great damage in a short space of time.

Both reformist and radical greens could find evidence to support their case in the decade after the Rio Earth Summit. The green movement had been central to the promotion of global environmental problems as a central challenge for the modern world. However the 'balance sheet' drawn up for the UN's follow-up meeting ten years on was less positive. The World Summit on Sustainable Development (WSSD), held in Johannesburg, South Africa, in September 2002, suggested that society had made very little meaningful progress in meeting the challenge of integrating environment, economy and society.

The green movement has a lot of work to do to bind their ideas into the heart of mainstream politics and economics. The next part of this book will look at some of the ideas that have shaped different wings of the movement and go further into a discussion of the implications of climate change for environmental politics. It will also explore the ways in which the greens are redrawing the boundaries of politics.

2

What makes greens different?

There is growing acceptance of the green movement's case on environmental change amongst senior government and business figures and the public. Surely the greens' work is done, and they can, in the words of one longstanding green activist 'go back to pruning the roses'?

No. The green movement's work is about much more than pointing to problems. It is also about pointing to the deeper transformations demanded of society once environmental problems have been acknowledged. Common to all green politics is a sense that existing frameworks – be they intellectual, political or cultural – are incomplete or inadequate. Looking through a green lens demands a fundamental rethinking of interests, responsibilities. It demands a big shake-up of what we think of as the proper subjects of ethics and politics. In what follows I will try to pick out a few of the most prominent names and concepts in green thinking together with some of the chief criticisms of these positions.

Deep ecology, social ecology and eco-feminism

The environmental movement of the late 1960s and early 1970s spawned new ways of looking at the world. All these have been forced to travel some distance from the main current of Western political thought in their attempts to remind society that it is part of, rather than separate from, the natural world.

'Deep ecology', a term first coined by Norwegian philosopher Arne Naess, has been particularly influential in North America. It starts from a 'vivid expression of deep concern for non-humans'[15] and represents a shift in the centre of gravity of political concern towards the non-human world.

It is a shift that Murray Bookchin, founder of a strand of green thinking known as 'social ecology', found naive, misanthropic and even dangerous. This former New York taxi driver and trades unionist placed a critique of the nature of social relations, and specifically hierarchy, at the hub of his argument about the roots of ecological degradation. Strongly influenced by anarchist and radical socialist traditions, Bookchin argued that the over-centralized state damaged both society and ecology. His solution was to propose human-scaled, self-governing municipalities, existing in confederations.

Bookchin viewed nature as being interdependent and egalitarian. He argued that there is no hierarchy within ecosystems: no 'kings of beasts' and no 'lowly ants'. This made it possible for Bookchin to claim that human societies are in fact naturally co-operative.

Deep and social ecology have often been presented as contrasting and conflicting theories. But how great is the distance between them? – or indeed the diverse body of variants that have sprung up since their introduction? Although combatants on either side of the argument have stressed their differences in the positions, the main originator of deep ecology plays these down. In his more recent writing, Naess argues that the deep ecology movement asks for extended and deep care for humans as well as non-humans. He agrees that what is distinctive about this position is the depth of concern for non-humans. This does not imply less concern for humans. Naess suggests that '(t)he term "deep" . . . refers to depth of premises motivating its supporters – and the depth of the social changes necessary to overcome the environmental crisis'.

DEEP ECOLOGY'S EIGHT POINTS

1 Every living being has intrinsic or inherent value (meaning they have value independent of the practical, economic or other value that might be assigned to them by human beings)

2 Richness and diversity of kinds of living beings have intrinsic or inherent value (i.e. biodiversity)

3 Humans have no right to reduce this richness and diversity except to satisfy vital human needs

4 A flourishing of human life and cultures is compatible with the decrease of the human population. The flourishing of nonhuman life requires such a decrease

5 Present human interference with the nonhuman world is excessive, and the situation is worsening

6 Policies must be changed in view of points one to five. These policies affect basic economic, technological and ideological structures

7 The appreciation of a high quality of life will supersede that of a high standard of living

8 Those who accept the foregoing points have an obligation to try to contribute directly or indirectly to the implementation of the necessary changes.[16]

Deep and social ecologists share a great deal in terms of both the problems that motivate them, and the vision of ecological and socially sustainable societies that they promote. They are also open to the same criticisms. Bookchin views the natural world as inherently cooperative, and the present state of society as a form of 'false consciousness'. He promises liberation through the subdivision of society into human-scale communities. This seems painfully idealistic, and at odds with the reality of political and cultural globalization. His insistence on radical decentralization and self-determination seem rather naive and hazardous in the face of a problem like climate change.

As to deep ecology's eight points, who will consider which living being has more 'intrinsic value' when their interests conflict? How will a decrease in human population be achieved, and who will decide what is and isn't a sustainable number? Who will define 'real human interests' or 'necessary changes'? How will disputes be resolved? If phrased clumsily, these ideas can leave the green movement too closely associated with authoritarianism. Their radical nature also threatens the greens with marginality and irrelevance. They seem to me to be disconnected from the daily life experiences of most people in the developed world (let alone the developing world). Embracing this thinking amounts to a retreat from the world of short-term deals and hard decisions into the twilight zone of radical rhetoric. The radicals' reply to this is that, at a time when the centre ground of politics proclaims 'we're all greens now', greens need to be carrying ecological debates to their radical conclusion.

There is another strand of intellectual innovation in the green movement that starts from a very different position: 'ecofeminism'. As with any movement, the greens have been shaped by their wider cultural milieu. The feminist movement has grown in parallel with environmentalism as a prominent feature of politics from the late 1960s to the present. Feminist critiques extended far beyond the day-to-day political realm and reached deep into the culture. It should be no surprise then to find that some theorists, tagged eco-feminists, have come to relate men's domination of women to its precursor, namely men's domination over nature. In other words, patriarchy in society is an extension of patriarchy in nature. Val Plumwood argues:

> Ecological feminists are involved in a great cultural revaluation of the status of women, the feminine and the natural, a revaluation which must recognise the way in which their historical connection in western culture has influenced the construction of feminine identity and . . . both masculine and human identity.[17]

Many feminists are critical of the tendency of some eco-feminists to seize upon the persistent cultural association of women and nature (earth goddesses; mother nature etc.) and argue that these kinds of link have frequently been used to oppress women. In reply, eco-feminists argue that there is a stark contrast between masculine culture and its values and the intertwined characteristics of women and non-human nature, specifically concerning nurturing. They argue that the life experiences of women bring them much closer to the rhythms of nature (primarily menstruation; and for mothers, pregnancy and lactation).

Eco-feminism found a new emphasis in the writing of the Indian biologist and activist, Vandana Shiva. She adds into the equation the dominance of the developing world by the developed countries, giving particular emphasis to the invisibility of the work that women do and the essential services that ecology provides. These invisible contributions sustain everything from the local economy to all life on earth, and the material wealth which results. Such contributions of work and wealth are 'invisible' because they are closely tuned to specific local ecosystems and needs. Shiva notes that the more successful this work is in sustaining vital ecological processes, the more invisible it becomes.

Most critics of eco-feminism focus on the essentialism of the position, in other words the view that there is something inherent in women's nature that promotes them to a central role in resolving the environmental crisis. Contraception shows how women do not have to let nature dictate their destinies. Similarly the progress of women towards equal access to work outside the home and shared parenting suggest that the gendering of these activities in the past is at least as much a feature of our culture as of our nature. Defending herself against the charge, Plumwood points to the fact that feminist, ecological and other liberation movements have a lot in common. She insists her argument is based on a philosophy which seeks to 'challenge the existing order very deeply, and fundamentally at many levels'.[18]

A different critique is laid at the door of Vandana Shiva's position. Her views about women, nature and development have attracted criticism for their idealized portrayal of women's lives in traditional village communities. The reality, some development workers and specialists argue, is one of sustained hard labour and poverty, which a degree of Western-style development would do much to alleviate.

Whatever the criticisms of some branches of eco-feminism, this perspective remains a valued and energizing strand in green politics. Eco-feminists have argued that women's experience of oppression brings far more than their biology to green thought. Also, the fact remains that much environmental activism, particularly in the developing world, is driven by the specific concerns and perspectives of women.

Deep and social ecologists and eco-feminists have helped to shape the intellectual landscape of the green movement. They have taken greens beyond single-issue campaigning, and provoked many people to explore the radical consequences of bringing ecology into political life. But they haven't provided arguments of a scale or force that might deliver a revolution in world view. Some greens believe that that can only be found at the planetary level. Enter the Gaia hypothesis or Earth systems theory.

Thinking of the earth as a system

What distinguishes the Gaia hypothesis is that it starts from a scientific rather than a philosophical or political premise. A century of environmental science research has revealed the complex and interrelated processes of the natural world. This work has been influential in the intellectual development of the green movement for over a century. One of the most challenging thinkers in this field is the climate scientist, James Lovelock. Together with biologist Lynn Margulis he proposed an extraordinarily ambitious and controversial scientific hypothesis. The Gaia or Earth systems hypothesis provides intellectual underpinning for an ecocentric approach to politics and suggests that the Earth is an integrated and self-regulating organism where, in Lovelock's words:

the entire range of living matter on earth, from whales to viruses, and from oaks to algae, could be regarded as a single living entity, capable of manipulating the earth's atmosphere to suit its overall needs.[19]

This offers the greens a new paradigm, or way of thinking. Gaia is defined as a complex entity made up of multiple feedbacks between biosphere, atmosphere, oceans and soil, amounting to a system that seeks 'an optimum physical and chemical environment for life on this planet'.[20] It is a hypothesis which has been dismissed by many in the science community as unverifiable and exaggerated. Few professional scientists have been comfortable with a term that has also been associated with what they see as the mystic quackery peddled by the fringes of the green movement.

Nevertheless many scientists acknowledge that the basic principles of 'biogeochemistry' or 'Earth systems science' provide a solid framework for thinking about the complexities of global environmental change. Gaia theory has also helped develop political thinking about environmental problems. The philosopher Mary Midgley sees it as a means of correcting three hundred years of distortion in the way political philosophy has represented humankind's relationship with nature. She suggests Lovelock should be seen as progressing the work of Copernicus and Darwin. Gaia theory helps to dismantle humanity's conviction in its own separateness from, and sovereignty over, nature. It offers a more realistic way of understanding not just the Earth, but also ourselves as its inhabitants. She suggests that:

The idea of Gaia – of life on earth as a self-sustaining natural system – is a powerful tool that could generate solutions to many of our current problems. It does not just lead to new applications of science and technology. It can also counteract the corrosive forms of social atomism and individualism that infuse much current scientific thought. Its approach, once fully grasped, makes a profound difference, not just to how we see the earth but to how we understand life and ourselves.[21]

Although the work has been applied crudely by some greens, and is occasionally hitched to dubious enviro-mysticism, Lovelock himself doesn't fall into such traps. In response to those greens who argue that we should act as 'stewards' of the earth, Lovelock quips that we are more like its 'shop stewards': our task is not so much to care for the rest of life but rather to act as its most articulate representatives.

It is not just his placing of humans within a living system that is powerful: it is also the way Lovelock disrupts conventional thinking about 'the way nature is'. One of the reasons Mary Midgley identifies Lovelock's ideas as important is that they correct an overemphasis on competition that has resulted from what she views as a false reading of Darwinism. Sociobiology has been used to justify competitiveness in all things – including economy and the use of natural resources. Midgley finds in Gaia arguments which suggest that cooperation is at least as important as competition. She sees it is an idea of sufficient force and integrity to start to bring green thinking to centre stage.

At the time when Lovelock first presented his ideas to fellow scientists in 1969 it was daring, even imprudent, for an established scientist to suggest that the earth operated as one living entity. It was Lovelock's work with NASA, researching the possibility of life on Mars, that had inspired him to look back at the nature of life on earth in a new, more complete and systematic way. By the end of the 1980s Lovelock and colleagues were no longer alone in thinking in planetary terms. An emerging scientific consensus on the possibility of global climate changes caused by human activity was entering public debate, giving new life and potency to green ideas.

What does climate change mean for green politics?

The UN environment and development conferences of 1992 and 2002 appeared to confirm that global environmental change issues – climate change and biodiversity loss – had become widely recognized by political leaders as urgent and important. So: is there anything left for greens to do? Greens argue that their voice needs to be heard now more than ever before. Their approach to climate change, probably the issue that has given the greens more prominence and legitimacy than any other, explains why.

Greens believe that climate change takes the environment to the centre of political debate. This is a grand claim at a time when so many other issues demand attention. Certainly climate change connects to so many pressing issues: it affects migration, food security, the political economy of energy, poverty and development, and the nature of global governance. But it is precisely the fact that it is so interconnected and complex that has made it so difficult to act on.

Green politics has benefited from harvesting the results of an immense scientific review of the issue of climate change that has gone on over the last fifteen years. A focused international research effort since the late 1980s has shown that a number of gases have the potential to contribute to what is often termed anthropogenically (i.e. human-)induced climate change. (The term anthropogenic is used to acknowledge that climate changes and the 'greenhouse effect' are naturally occurring processes, and also that the climate can be changed by the release into the atmosphere of, above all, carbon dioxide, methane, chlorofluorocarbons (CFCs: the gases that are also associated with the destruction of the ozone layer) and nitrous oxide.) The main climate-forcing gas is carbon dioxide, produced by the burning of fossil fuels such as coal and gas. Economic development, largely fuelled by these energy sources, is ensuring that emissions are growing fast. Globally averaged surface temperature is one of the key measurements that this debate focuses on. The IPCC predicted in its last report that this is likely to increase by between 1.4 and 5.8°C to the year 2100.[22] While even the higher estimates of temperature increases don't immediately appear alarming to temperate developed-world countries, climate change specialists have shown that the consequences could be far-reaching and overwhelmingly negative.

Their findings revive something of the mood of the unfulfilled catastrophe predictions of the proto-greens of the late 1960s and early 1970s, and have brought an energy and urgency to the green movement as a whole. The IPCC's 2001 Third Assessment Report is worded cautiously – as one would expect from a scientific peer-review process. But there is a key comment at the heart of their work: 'an increasing body of observations gives a collective picture of a warming world and other changes in the climate system'. The report goes on to portray the causes and very serious consequences of climate change.

To bring the reality of climate change to life two US bodies, the Union of Concerned Scientists and the World Resources Institute, have developed a regularly updated climate change 'hot map'.[23] The map shows 'fingerprints' of climate change that indicate evidence of widespread and long-term trends towards warmer global temperatures. They also show 'harbingers', that is, events

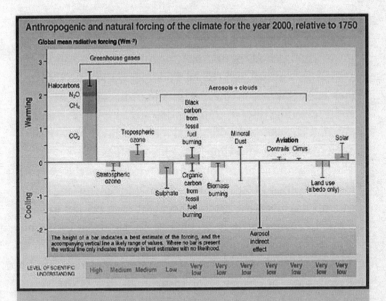

Anthropogenic and natural forcing of the climate for the year 2000, relative to 1750

Source:
www.ipcc.ch/present/graphics/2001syr/small/06.01.jpg,
accessed by author at 3/12/05

Pick out just three things from this chart. First note the summary of greenhouse gases identified with warming. CO_2 is the most significant, but the others are also increasing due to human activity. Notice also the indication of level of scientific understanding at the bottom; from high to very low. Finally, this illustration is useful for showing that it is known that there are also cooling factors. Making sense of how the climate system works is a major challenge – predicting the impact of human activity on the climate over the next hundred years is far more complex.

that illustrate the sorts of impact that promise to be more frequent and widespread with continued warming. Fingerprints include: heatwaves and periods of unusually warm weather; ocean warming, a rise in sea level and coastal flooding; glaciers melting and higher temperatures in the Arctic and Antarctic. Harbingers include: spreading disease; earlier spring arrival; plant and animal population changes and shifts; coral reef bleaching; heavy downpours, snowfalls, and flooding, droughts and fires.

The main source of carbon dioxide emissions is the burning of fossil fuels such as oil and gas, primarily for energy and transport. This has given the green movement their central mission on climate change: that is, to chart a course to an economic system that is not dependent on carbon.

Three main factors influence emissions: population, wealth and technological change. Not surprisingly the USA, with a large population, a high per capita GDP, and the world's most energy-intensive lifestyle, is the world's biggest polluter. Since the late 1990s, US politicians have refused to take political risks that threaten the American public's resource-hungry way of life. This stance has made the US government the target of intense criticism by the American and global green movement.

Although developed-world economies are responsible for the great bulk of historic and current emissions, many developing countries are catching up fast. One of the most politically charged facts in climate negotiations is that developing-country emissions are increasing five times faster than those in the industrialized world. They are soon set to make up the majority of global emissions. Leading US negotiators and Republican politicians have been keen to point out that as China and India develop, it will become just as important that they 'decarbonize' their economy.

The central feature of any climate change programme is the reversal of trends in the burning of fossil fuels. This goal is at the

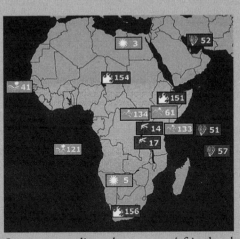

Source: www.climatehotmap.org/africa.html

This clickable Internet-published map demonstrates the value of the web as a fast cheap means of communicating the complexity of climate change. For example, the numbered boxes refer to:

Fingerprints:

61 Kenya – Mt Kenya's largest glacier disappearing. 92% of the Lewis Glacier has melted in the past 100 years.

121 World Ocean – Warming water. The world ocean has experienced a net warming of 0.11°F (0.06°C) from the sea surface to a depth of 10,000 feet (3,000 m) over the past 35–45 years . . . Warming is occurring in all ocean basins and at much deeper depths than previously thought.

Harbingers:

17 Tanzania – Malaria expands in mountains. Higher annual temperatures in the Usamabara Mountains have been linked to expanding malaria transmission.

51 Indian Ocean – Coral Reef Bleaching (includes Seychelles; Kenya; Reunion; Mauritius; Somalia; Madagascar; Maldives; Indonesia; Sri Lanka; Gulf of Thailand [Siam]; Andaman Islands; Malaysia; Oman; India; and Cambodia).[24]

core of the Kyoto Protocol, drafted after protracted international negotiation, with a wording agreed in December 1997, which seeks to create a framework for a worldwide reduction in carbon emissions. The Kyoto Protocol is a 'living' agreement, and the parties that have signed up to this programme meet regularly to monitor progress and consider needs for new measures.

Greens criticize the Kyoto target of a 5% reduction on 1990 levels by 2012 as lacking ambition. They argue (as do increasing numbers of senior scientists) that cuts of between 60–90% of emissions by 2050 are necessary to stabilize the climate. They also argue that politicians in the developed world are failing to promote the switch to a non-fossil fuel economy. Greens have also pressed the question of why there is so little commitment to helping the developing world to 'leapfrog' over fossil-fuel based economic development. The greens place renewable energy and energy efficiency centre stage. These goals would be pursued – echoing Schumacher's teaching – via 'appropriate' community-controlled technology choices. This last point is important in their argument against nuclear energy as a response to climate change.[25]

The issue of climate change has given new life and legitimacy to some long-established green goals. But it also presents tactical and strategic challenges. Should they enter day-to-day debate and win some short-term victories? Is there a need for a more radical voice distanced from political horse-trading that can give society a more accurate and more urgent sense of its choices? The diverse branches of the green movement are currently attempting to cover both options, and all points in between.

Greens approach the politics of climate change by calling attention to the simple fact that the impacts will be felt most dramatically in the developing world although the great majority of the polluting has been committed in the developed world. A Westerner taking a short-haul holiday flight is responsible for the same greenhouse gas emissions as a typical Bangladeshi for a year. Our industrial development has been bought at the cost of the stability of the current and future climate. The consequences of this will be felt most by those who have benefited least from the carbon-fed industrial revolution and post-war economic boom.

Few greens today would argue with the simple formula first proposed by green economists such as Barry Commoner in the 1970s. He calculated environmental impact as the product of three factors – population, multiplied by the amount of an economic good per capita multiplied by the output of pollutant per unit of the economic good produced. Sometimes labelled 'steady-state economics' this approach pointed to how technology and a movement towards stable human numbers could work together to lighten the human load on the biosphere.

Environmentalists in the 1970s were primarily concerned with rapid population growth at a time when population was static or declining in the developed world. This laid them open to charges of 'eco-fascism'. Developing-world commentators and leaders condemned rich-world environmentalists with the jibe that, now that economic development had delivered a good standard of living, they wanted to 'pull the ladder up' behind them and condemn the developing world to a state of perpetual underdevelopment.

Pressure of human numbers remains a key problem. But it is now widely recognized in the green movement that clumsily introduced contraception programmes not only contradict other dimensions of green ideology (self-determination and grassroots decision-making) but are also ineffective. Greens now argue first for improvements in women's literacy levels and in primary and preventive healthcare. More emphasis is now put on the dramatic disparity between consumption per capita in the developed world and the developing world. The issue is no longer about raw human numbers, but about lifestyles and consumption.

Most of the emissions responsible for human-induced climate change can be traced to the developed world, with its fossil-fuel based lifestyles and systems. These include the private car, resource-intensive food systems, and a constant pursuit of novelty and convenience. Much of the greens' concern with the environmental hazards presented by increasing human numbers has been shifted towards reducing the environmental impact of populations in the developed world. This approach does more than neutralize the charges of 'eco-fascism' that the greens have faced in the past. Equity becomes the starting point for thinking about human numbers and needs, environmental change and material intensity of lifestyle. This will matter more by the day, as the fast-growing middle classes of India and China seek to mimic the resource-hungry consumption patterns of the developed world.

The issue of climate change gives force to the 1970s environmentalist slogan 'Think global, act local'. At last green ideas seem to be at the heart of political debate.

Rethinking the boundaries of politics

Or are they? Surely the measure of political ideas is not whether they are talked about but whether they change things? Deep and social ecology, eco-feminism and Gaia theory are hardly on the lips of the general public. In fact they rarely register as terms and concepts in the day-to-day work of the green movement.

Do the greens have the potential not just to describe the world's problems, but also to solve them?

Greens have tried to stretch the boundaries of what we think of as political and who and what we think about in ethical terms. Greens want to find ways of ensuring that future generations, 'distant others' (i.e. people distant in space or time) and the non-human natural world all get represented in today's decisions.

There is nothing new in the greens' insistence that we should consider the interests of the poor. But the greens are unique in arguing that the inter-connectedness of fate of humans and their environments demands that we bring the non-human world into our ethics and politics. This way of thinking has begun to appear in mainstream political debates around not only climate change, but also the protection of species and their habitats. It is finding expression in both planning legislation and guidance at the most local level, and climate change policy construction at the national and international level. After decades of designing settlements around the private car, planners in Europe and North America are trying to encourage the development of cities and towns in such a way as to reduce the need to travel. Plans to protect and increase biodiversity – in cities as well as rural areas – are increasingly stitched into medium-term planning. Building and other regulations are improving the energy efficiency of new and existing buildings. While some of these developments are the result of far-sighted local authorities and pressure from local green groups, much of it is the direct result of national and international environmental agreements.

Green thinking has also permeated some mainstream thinking about the concept of security. The dominant notion of human security in the second half of the twentieth century was founded in a doctrinaire 'realism' that assumed nations would always try to maximize their own narrow interests. This was achieved via diplomacy backed up, in the case of the super-powers, by the capacity to inflict unimaginable damage through conventional and nuclear arms.

The green movement's perspective on security was forged in this context, and closely allied to that of the peace movement. In a step back from the doom-laden promises of imminent catastrophe in the 1970s, present-day greens are more likely to draw attention to vulnerable human populations, habitats under threat and the consequences for human society as a whole.

They also point to how threats to essential natural resources such as productive land, clean water or fuel can be found at the root of many conflicts, such as those in the Middle East and North Africa. They argue, for example, that deforestation does not just carry cultural and local economic costs. The loss of bio-diversity may shut off potentially important new drug and nutritional breakthroughs, and hence threaten long-term human security worldwide. Greens have also pointed to how climate change threatens widespread and unpredictable disruptions to settlements and food systems and, in turn, may result in large-scale human migrations.

Green thinking begins with the assumption that the natural environment is the fundamental basis of all human security. For greens, solving international environmental problems is viewed as a starting point for international collaboration on a range of foreign policy challenges.

This combines with their long-established views on technology and democracy to shape a distinctive take on peace and defence. They have consistently aligned themselves with the peace movement and against international arms trade and

NATO. The greens' approach to security borrows much from Gandhi's teaching, above all in their insistence on the need to look at the root causes of conflict – above all, fuel, water and food insecurity. Ensuring these is both more humane and cost-effective than sustained investments in armed defence. It is a position which has been gaining ground amongst some of the more imaginative defence strategists as the frequency and intensity of resource-based conflicts increase around the world.

The green view on security is linked to their approach to science, technology and risk-taking. The green movement has always had an ambivalent relationship with science and technology. Scientific findings have provided the bedrock for their claims of ecological crisis, and the application of technology has long been central to their charting of a new course for society. At the same time greens have argued that some central features of the Western scientific tradition have contributed to the ecological crisis. They have consistently looked for a radically different approach in the handling of scientific findings and the introduction of new technology.

This is expressed in the principle that first emerged in West Germany in the 1970s, termed the *Vorsorgeprinzip* or 'precautionary principle'. It became accepted as a principle of German environmental law, and has lodged itself gradually in international and national environmental policy debates. It appears as a foundation for some European Union legislation and UN agreements. The principal aim is to shift the burden of proof from those that argue that a particular activity or plan carries a risk to those that are engaging in or proposing the activity. An authoritative expression of the principle is the Wingspread Statement, drafted by an international group of academics and environmental campaigners in 1998, which proposed that:

When an activity raises threats of harm to the environment or human health, precautionary measures should be taken even if some cause and effect relationships are not fully established scientifically.[26]

On paper the precautionary principle has already found its way into mainstream policy development. It features in some European Union institutional protocols and policies and has influenced the decisions of some major companies. The precautionary principle dictates the green response to emerging technologies such as genetically modified (GM) and nanotech, and to longer fought battles over nuclear power. The principle neatly meshes their thinking about the new boundaries of ethical responsibility and their future-oriented politics. It has created a policy tool that brings their perspective on risk-taking and economic development into near-term policy decisions.

The call from greens for wider definitions of security is attracting interest in surprising quarters, including the military and scientific establishments. Their take on precaution also seems to be catching the public mood. But there are some hazards in their approach. The scale of environmental and social challenges seems to demand that human societies apply all their creativity to problem-solving. But the greens' stance on risk may slow or halt experiments and innovation across the board. By cloaking society in the precautionary principle, greens may choke off some areas of research and development that could bring rich rewards in terms of environmental and human security in key areas including energy, transport or agriculture. For this reason greens are often dismissed in the research community as 'Luddite' and superstitious. In terms of science and technology, promoting carefully designed but imaginative experiment and innovation may result in important breakthroughs. At the same time, rigid 'preservationism' of the countryside or cities could halt debate about what the relationship between cities and countryside should be, and denies the inherent dynamism of both the natural and social worlds, and the relationship between them.

A more sophisticated green view on precaution is that life science research or technology on a very small scale (codes for, among other things, GM and nanotechnology) may not in themselves be harmful. It is the way they are commissioned, owned and applied that carries the greater threat. Greens could emphasize that it is the secretive corporate ownership of some of these technologies, and the undemocratic and centralized nature of much risk decision-making that may generate environmentally damaging outcomes. This would allow them to refresh their relationship with science and technology, and commit the green movement to a forward-looking tone of curiosity, experiment and invention.

3

How can green thinking change the world?

Some aspects of green thinking have travelled a surprisingly long way in a short space of time. There is a sense of opportunity in the air. What would it mean if green ideas were taken up? How have greens sought to map an ecologically and socially sustainable future for society? In this section I am going to look at their distinctive and interlocking views on democracy, technology, economics and, ultimately, the way they define progress. I will also make a little space for a return to the issue of whether it still holds that 'the personal is political' for the greens, and consider whether greens think that individual actions still count as much as political change. I want to explore how coherent, consistent and viable their political philosophy and programmes are. In short – can greens change the world?

Green democracy – can we survive in freedom?

Both friends and critics of the green movement have pointed to a central challenge: how can society implement the changes that greens demand while preserving treasured democratic principles? Can human societies survive yet still enjoy the individual freedoms that are integral to democratic living? Critics of both left and right have consistently laid the charge of authoritarianism at the door of the greens. They see their radical programmes of economic and social transformation as requiring a highly interventionist state. There is a small minority of greens who propose draconian measures, it is true; but by far the strongest impulse within the green movement is towards the nurturing of grassroots democracy.

It is difficult to separate out the philosophical and practical sources of this commitment, and the balance between the two varies across the movement. Some refer to the longstanding failures and injustices delivered by state structures, and argue that dispensing with political hierarchies is a prerequisite for an environmentally sustainable society. Those influenced by deep ecology go a step further to propose social organization on a scale dictated by the natural boundaries of a bio-region (marked out, for example, by a watershed). The community of that bio-region would, it is argued, be able to sustain itself on the basis of the resources within it, so it follows that political questions should also be debated within that area. The feminist and peace movements of the 1970s and 1980s were another politically and philosophically rooted source of commitment to grassroots or participative democracy, that has fed into green political thought.

But most greens are more pragmatic than ideological. They argue that decentralized decision-making is, in practical terms, the best way of negotiating the journey to a sustainable society. They also suggest that wider participation in debate leads to a much greater degree of commitment and support for a chosen course of action, making it much more likely that the implementation phase of any policy will enjoy success.

The green perspective on democracy connects directly with green views on science and technology. Greens point to nuclear power and genetically modified (GM) foods as the products of over-centralized decisions made in the interests of profit of major companies. They work to expose the vanity of a scientific paradigm that is losing contact with wider society. Greens propose to extend the democratization of policy and politics into the worlds of science and technology in order to counteract the influence of business in these areas. Public reactions to GM and other food scandals, and the evidence of a rapid decline in public trust in institutions, have lent support to the green case. Questions remain about the greens' approach to democracy. What is the appropriate scale and speed of decision-making? How can the public be equipped with sufficient understanding to make judgements about very complex science or technology? Despite tensions and inconsistencies, greens seem close to the public mood on trust and risk.

Green technology – more than 'alternative'?

The green stance on risk and democracy is shaped in part by their response to things they are against. Green thinking about technology gives them a chance to show something that they are *for*. The 'new limits to growth', marked out by climate change and accelerating loss of biodiversity, are no less alarming than those outlined in the early 1970s. But the green movement's responses are now more measured, and suggest they have learnt from past failures. Many environmentalists in the early 1970s believed that an 'ecotopia' might be delivered by the application of radical technologies. Present-day greens have tended to be more cautious in their claims and more thoughtful in placing technology within its social context.

Green thinking is reshaping design and technology. Talk of sustainable manufacturing and green design has reached deep into higher education and professional engineering and design bodies. But can technology on its own offer solutions to environmental problems? Greens try to set proposed 'techno-fixes' within their social contexts, and stress what else is needed to allow them to be effective.

Changing views of green technology are nicely illustrated by the status of renewable energy sources, for a long time referred to as 'alternative' energy. In the 1970s and 1980s some radical greens promoted technology as the foundation of an environmentally sustainable society, and small-scale renewables were prominent in this.

One of the most celebrated figures in the green technology Hall of Fame is Buckminster Fuller, whose geodesic domes gave physical form to a way of thinking about the future. These buildings were low energy in terms of both construction and use, while their startling and futuristic design suggested to enthusiasts that society could, with enough imagination, design its way out of the environmental crisis. Similarly, many people were inspired to build their own ecological homes. One popular resource was architect Walter Segal's self-build system. Segal insisted his was an approach to building that could empower people rather than impose a design upon them. Modular timber-frame units allowed rapid and low-skill construction of comfortable, cheap homes. They can be found all over the world, and are still being drawn on by community and self-builders thirty years on. The hallmarks of what could be called a green ideology of design were emerging. This included grassroots participation in the design process, independence from expertise, low-energy demands in the construction and life of a product, reusability/recyclability and adaptability to changing circumstances and needs.

The work of people like Segal and Fuller were some of the central attractions in publications like the groundbreaking *Whole Earth Catalog*, first published in the USA in 1968. This bizarre compendium was a toolkit for alternative ways of living and thinking. Every page offered a jumbled collage of advice and small business adverts on anything from chicken-raising to sexual technique. That it was a publishing triumph indicated that there was a movement out there. That it was a perplexing blend of high-concept design and woodcraft lore showed that this was a diverse movement that didn't have a clear idea of where its boundaries lay.

Projects like the *Whole Earth Catalog* signalled the growth of experimental communities working to implement alternative technology and ways of living. They were mostly short lived. A small number of governments, particularly in Scandinavia, invested in energy conservation and renewable energy technologies from the 1970s onwards. But these were the exception. When low oil prices and easy availability returned in the late 1970s, green thinking on technology lost its opportunity to enter the mainstream.

However, the steady growth in both numbers and influence of the green movement in the 1980s and early 1990s brought a change in fortunes for some aspects of greens' views on technology. By the mid-1990s there was increasingly widespread public concern at climate change. Fuel security and pollution problems created a much more powerful body of support for renewable (no longer 'alternative') energy and other green approaches to technology.

There are some influential thinkers whose biographies demonstrate this journey from margins to mainstream. The American Amory Lovins had been a star of the alternative technology and radical environmentalist scene since the late 1960s.

In the 1990s Lovins and his partner L. Hunter Lovins worked with, among others, the German Ernst von Weizsacker to demonstrate how business can easily improve its productivity by a factor of four without increasing its environmental footprint. Their Factor Four proposal, based entirely on tested and existing technologies, provoked business on its own terms: 'Why tolerate such waste? – It's expensive and threatens the long-term sustainability of your business.' The Lovins enjoyed luring audiences in the 1990s into a new way of thinking about energy and design by boasting about the bananas grown in their highly efficient home and workplace in the Rocky Mountains. Amory Lovins would provoke the car industry with an outline of an ultra-lightweight hybrid electric 'hypercar' that could be built with existing technology.

'Factor Four' means that resource productivity can – and should – grow fourfold. The amount of wealth extracted from one unit of natural resource can quadruple. Thus we can live twice as well – yet use half as much. That message is both novel and simple.[27]

The principle of assessing the whole life cycle of a product, with its environmental impact central to the assessment, has become fundamental to best practice in environmental management. Some corporations, from car to clothing manufacturers, have started to integrate such principles, helped by a growing army of green business consultants. The 'whole life-cycle thinking' that greens pioneered has reached beyond technology and design. It is now applied to analysis of whole chains of production and consumption in fields such as timber and fisheries, and car and carpet manufacturing. Full and critical reporting of social and environmental performance by business (sometimes known as Corporate Social Responsibility or CSR reporting), alongside their reporting of financial results, is seen as a crucial complement to technological innovations. Such reporting can give the business itself, critics, the media and wider society the opportunity to benchmark performance, particularly of global companies. It allows green and social movements to maintain surveillance of those industries with a major environmental impact, and to keep advancing the baseline of environmental and social acceptability.

There are areas where governments have sought to promote the development and growth of green technologies. Japan, Germany and government bodies in the USA have all started on ambitious solar roof schemes. These kinds of programme are aimed at 'technology forcing': in other words, developing a market for new products and services by introducing incentives.

All this is a long way from the solitary experimental wind turbines and prototype solar roofs that (sometimes) powered the utopian experiments of alternative communities in the 1970s. The presence of major corporations in the delivery of the greens' technological pipe dreams raises difficult questions for a movement that had anticipated a very different route to a 'solar economy'. The most promising signs that human societies are approaching a renewables-based economy don't rely on a mushrooming of autonomous grassroots projects by radical greens. Instead they are based on the policies, research and capital investments made by governments and powerful companies. The green movement has in some cases been directly involved in these developments. Greenpeace has worked with the solar arms of the oil industry to demonstrate the potential of renewables, and in the UK has worked with the electricity industry to establish a market for wind-generated electricity.

This all seems a long way from Schumacher's 'small is beautiful' dictum, but reflects the fact that the world's biggest companies have a longer reach into consumer choice and thinking than governments. They have the capacity to transform the manner of production, use and disposal of their products and services more speedily than any social movement. At first sight this line of argument implies that the greens have become redundant. It makes more sense to acknowledge that the green movement's constant pressure on government and business over three decades has been a necessary, albeit not sufficient, basis for these changes. Does this mean that the green ideology of design and technology that evolved in the 1970s is no longer relevant? In fact many greens have not been arguing that small is always beautiful. It sounds less snappy, but what they've really been saying is that technology must be applied to social needs and within ecological constraints.

Where will this debate go next, and what role will greens play? The rapid economic development of, for example, India and China make this an urgent question. The most populous countries on the planet have rapidly growing resource-hungry middle classes. Green technologists such as Von Weizsacker and the Lovins have argued that their proposed 'Factor Four' improvements will be inadequate even if they can be achieved soon if there is fast growth in demand for energy-hungry goods and services. They argue that resource productivity in fact needs to increase by a factor of ten in developed-world industries and economies if equitable economic development and ecological sustainability is to be achieved. This would require a far more radical rethinking of the way technology, resources and processes are applied to meet society's goals. Greens will need to work quickly if their arguments about new priorities and practices in design, production and consumption are to have any influence. Some of the biggest developing-world economies are already some way down the fossil-fuelled fast-lane to economic development.

Green thinking about energy supply and use, life cycles, and 'whole-systems' thinking is entering the mainstream. But it has not gained a firm grip on most businesses and governments. The emergence of mature and cost-effective energy conservation and renewable energy technologies all set the scene for rapid shifts towards environmentally sustainable industrial production. But clearly there is a missing ingredient. The robust and timely green arguments about technology are not bringing about rapid change. The great majority of business and government actions do not reflect 'Factor Four' thinking let alone 'Factor Ten' thinking. The green movement has learnt the hard way that it is not enough to demonstrate how green technology can go from the drawing board to production. Greens have recognized that the most important step will be the more politically challenging one of transforming the economic signals felt at local, national and global levels.

Putting the 'eco' back into economics

The growth fetish, while on balance quite useful in a world with empty land, shoals of undisturbed fish, vast forests, and a robust ozone shield, helped create a more crowded and stressed one. Despite the appearance of ecological buffers and mounting real costs, ideological lock-in reigned in both capitalist and communist circles ... Economic thought did not adjust to the changed conditions it helped to create; thereby it continued to legitimate, and indeed indirectly to cause, massive and rapid ecological change. The overarching priority of economic growth was easily the most important idea of the twentieth-century.[28]

McNeill's environmental history of the twentieth century confirms the greens' view that economic growth is the prime source of environmental problems. At the same time many also believe economic tools to be central to any solution. Greens are in a position to remind society of a simple but often forgotten truth: that the economy is a human artefact and that society can take it and shape it according to its priorities. This seemingly modest starting point may yet prove to be a very powerful one. The argument is being put at a time when society seems increasingly in thrall to the pursuit of economic growth at the cost of local communities and the global climate.

The fact that a narrow and particular view of economics dominates the modern world has not been lost on the greens. They widely identify the all-consuming obsession of mainstream politics with Gross Domestic Product (GDP), a single figure that aims to summarize a country's economic performance, as the source of many environmental ills. For example green economist Herman Daly has dubbed GDP 'a statistically graven image of Mammon'.[29] Above all greens point out that almost all economic thinking fails to acknowledge the reliance of human economies upon the biophysical systems that underpin all life.

But at the same time some greens draw hope from the very fact that economics has a strong grip on society and politics. They see in it the potential for a dramatic transformation of society: if you can change economics you can change the world. Going back to basics, greens often observe that both ecology and economics share the root 'eco', from the Greek *oikos* meaning house, home or habitat. Both an *oikonomia* and an *oikologia* suggest a system of interacting, interdependent units. This illustrates green economists' willingness to take back some of the powerful tools that are currently deployed in the pursuit of a narrowly defined version of economic success.

The emergence of the green movement has been important both in nourishing new thinking in economics and helping create the political conditions needed to take some of these ideas into mainstream political debate. Environmental economists work within the neo-classical tradition. This views society as a mass of individuals all seeking to maximize their own (material) welfare. In this work environmental quality and protection becomes part of the job of defining the many aspects of human welfare.

When the surge in environmental concern in the 1970s drew economists to look at how markets were failing the environment, they used the language of costs. Pollution of any form is a cost – to the environment and society – but for most of the history of industrial society these costs were not reflected in the prices paid for goods and services. Since the 1970s environmental economists have gained ground with the argument that these unpaid costs – termed 'externalities' – should be brought into any calculation of financial costs. In other words externalities such as local air or water pollution should become internalized in the mainstream economy. It is a more economically efficient way of reducing environmental pollution than blunt and cumbersome regulation, as it forces the polluter to pay the costs of its action, making it irrational to harm the environment. This has usually been expressed in terms of arriving at valuations for costs of environmental damage and then expressing these costs via taxation or charges.

Greens have long promoted this 'polluter pays' principle, although they have usually pressed for it to be applied in tandem with tough regulation. Championing such market measures has helped greens to engage with recent economic debates in many parts of the world.

Green taxation has also offered the movement a way of

defending itself against the persistent charge laid by trade unionists that they favour 'trees more than jobs'. It also helps answer employers who fear that they want to run industry into the ground with costly environmental measures. For thirty years greens have argued for a shift from taxing work and business profits to taxing resources. In other words they are not proposing environmental taxation as an additional burden. Green taxation is about reducing tax on 'goods' such as work and enterprise and raising revenue against social and environmental 'bads', e.g. the use of climate-threatening fossil fuels and habitat-threatening mining. Such taxation helps to create a virtuous green cycle, that can accelerate innovation in and take-up of green technologies. Green economics is not just about industry. More complete price signals would go out to consumers of resource-intensive products and these would propel them towards greener choices.

But the greens have also been the first to point out the limitations of environmental economics. First, there are no perfect markets in the real world. Environmental and social harm is difficult – often impossible – to quantify. The economists who assign figures to externalities are not all-seeing gods, but frail humans. They will make decisions that reflect inherited prejudices. Such economic calculations will also be shaped by the distribution of power in society. Even when the environment is being taken into account, an economist weighing up the costs and benefits of, for example, a new road or housing development on a green-field site will be influenced by a whole body of institutional, cultural and political factors. These have frequently swung a decision against environmental interests. Greens fear that the figures fed into a calculation about a new housing or road project will more often than not favour economic development at the cost of other less tangible or immediate gains. These might include a habitat for a rare species, a treasured landscape or the rather abstract notion of a perceived threat to the quality of life of future generations.

In debates about the role of environmental economics, greens have generally argued that there are values that cannot be expressed in monetary terms and that there are radical uncertainties that cannot be factored into even the most sophisticated calculations.

A new branch of economics has grown up that is more closely attuned to green thinking. Ecological economists argue that environmental economists see the world as made up of rational actors making decisions in properly functional markets. Ecological economics draws on a much wider range of insights – including the physical laws of thermodynamics, ecology and environmental philosophy. While some environmental economics concepts are important in the greens' intellectual armoury, ecological economics does much more to extend green thinking in this critical area.

Although ecological economists are often treated as heretics within their profession, they are generally trained in neoclassical economics and can talk its language. This makes them much more effective critics than the great majority of greens who lack a foundation in economic theory. In truth 'economist' is a misleading term here. The range of disciplines contributing to this work is very broad and this can help ecologists as much as economists. John Proops summarizes this two-way exchange as follows:

Economists are increasingly coming to recognize that the study of human activities on a finite planet, in the long-run, requires a different set of concepts to those useful for the economic analysis of households, firms, and nation states in the short- and medium-run. In a complementary way, ecologists, and other natural scientists, are increasingly recognizing that economic activity is here to stay; human activities are coming to dominate the global ecosystem, and ecosystem analysis which does not explicitly include economic activities makes less and less sense.[30]

Ecological economics speaks to concerns that are central to the green movement. It recognizes environmental limits and expresses values concerning the non-human natural world and future generations. It also works for wide public participation in decision-making and offers a way of coping with the uncertainty that runs through so many environmental issues.

Perhaps the biggest contribution it can make is its potential to carry the greens' oft-repeated insights about biophysical limits directly into the lion's den of mainstream economics.

The simplest way of thinking about this is to consider the size of the economy relative to the ecosystem that contains it. In this account the economic world is a sub-system of the global ecosystem. This approach allows important questions to be asked about what the maximum scale of the economy might be. How far can it grow before the costs in terms of human welfare are intolerable? Herman Daly notes that the economy is, like an animal, a 'dissipative structure'; that is, it relies on a metabolic flow into and out of its system. These flows are often termed 'sources' and 'sinks'. Drawing on the laws of thermodynamics he notes that this flow begins with the depletion of useful resources from the environment and ends with the return of polluting wastes. So not only does our growing economy accelerate faster towards its ecosystem's inherent physical limits; it also pollutes it in the process. In other words, not only is it eroding the stock of possible resources, it is also destroying the capacity of the ecosystem to act as a sink.

Ecological economists argue that the interests of other humans (distant geographically or in time) and the non-human natural world must be made more explicit in decision-making. The way values are expressed in economic thought is crucial. Standard economics textbooks have an extremely limited notion of value. It is either expressed as a market value (a price), or a use value (expressed as willingness to pay for something or accept compensation for its loss). They also treat resources as belonging to the present. In a practice known as 'discounting', they discount the value of resources in the future compared with today.

Ecological economists have a much broader view of values and a much wider conception of equity. They are concerned to see the losses to future generations expressed alongside the gains to those of the present (in the rich world). We can see in this approach the origins of the Brundtland definition of sustainability. Some ecological economists also seek to represent non-monetary values (sometimes expressed as 'intrinsic' or existence values) of aspects of the non-human natural world; they also want to include the range of ecological goods and services that are not listed in standard economic accounting. They argue that economists must stop insisting on calculating everything according to notions of individual preferences and instead find ways of expressing collective values.

Ecological economists continue to stay close to ecological thinking when they get practical. They don't think there will be just a few dominant rules and methods in ecological economics. The inter-relationship between ecological and economic worlds is full of complexity. For that reason the abstract and novel idea of trying to express this range of values in economics calls for a new way of thinking. Ecological economics contrasts with conventional economics in keeping in view much longer timescales, or 'deep time'. Current shorter-term accounting practices could not be further from the approach of ecological economics. The latter works to integrate the generations, habitats, non-human species and landscapes of the long-term future.

Global environmental change and technologies such as nuclear energy or genetic modification may bring enormous costs to future generations and the non-human natural world. But despite widespread recognition of possible hazards, every-day decisions continue to focus on benefits in the present and the short term. The green movement's reasons for applying the precautionary principle in economics are nicely summarized by ecological economist, Robert Costanza:

> One does not run blindly through a dark landscape that may contain crevasses. One assumes they are there and goes gingerly and with eyes wide open, at least until one can see a little better.[31]

Green thinking on democracy, technology and economics, taken together, points to the need for a new set of priorities in our politics and economics. While this sentence reads simply enough, the practical implications are enormous. For there will need to be a substantial shift away from the current paradigm. A key battle that greens will need to win if this is to happen centres on societies' definition of 'progress'.

Redefining progress

Greens are far more than a bundle of single-issue agitators at the margins of politics. Despite their short history, they have already had a big influence on contemporary culture and politics. In addition to promoting their distinctive take on democracy, technology and economics, greens have provoked new ways of thinking about how we define quality and progress – whether in our national accounts, the way business is done, or in our daily lives.

Greens stress the need for humans to recognize their fundamental interconnectedness with, and reliance upon, natural systems. To capture people's imaginations, this simple but important fact needs to be expressed in a way that is intuitive and striking. Environmental or ecological 'footprinting' is designed to do just that. By considering together the resource needs, waste implications, technological context and ecological capacity of a given person, community, country, or even the planet as a whole, an ecological footprint can be calculated. This is a potentially rich way of communicating the concept of sustainability. An ecological footprint analysis summarizes both the intensity and equity of current resource use.

Humanity is held to have breached already the ecological capacity of the planet. The World Wide Fund for Nature (WWF's) 2004 *Living Planet* study provoked widespread media and public interest across the developed world with its finding that by 2050 we would need the equivalent of two more planet earths to support our resource-hungry lifestyles.[32] This approach can also be applied to individual regions or companies, so that, for example, it is possible to show a Californian town how it uses many times more resources than a similar-sized settlement in the developing world. The technique is blunt and has its critics. But the capacity to tailor communication about ecological hazards to widely varying groups – from schoolchildren to corporate bosses – makes it a powerful tool in furthering public understanding and debate.

Although footprinting has the potential to raise awareness of problems, it does little to help people move towards a more sustainable society or economy. With this need in mind, the greens have promoted the use of so-called sustainability indicators, above all by national governments. These represent a new way of expressing the economic, social and environmental state of a nation. Sustainability indicators were first proposed as an alternative to the narrow focus upon measures of economic growth. The greens' aim is to find a set of straightforward and intuitive measures of progress that can embody green economic, social and ecological principles. They are promoted as a way of measuring whether society is becoming more or less sustainable.

The greens' central insight is that there is an ecological basis to society and economy and that these three spheres must be considered together as an integrated whole. Evidence is building that may help to promote more integrated ways of thinking. Some of the most growth-obsessed nations are seeing some signs of changing attitudes to work, material reward, personal development and community. Some of the most-educated and affluent social groups on the planet are beginning to question the value of personal riches won at the cost of health or happiness. Increasing numbers of people are looking for other benchmarks of success.

There may be even more significant shifts going on within the business world. There is increasing recognition that the ecological costs of climate change, biodiversity/habitat loss and local pollution will return later to haunt corporations in the form of economic costs. Increasing numbers of business people are coming to recognize that the medium- and long-term stability of their own corporate fortunes could be threatened by environmental and social instability. The insurance industry today views climate change as one of the biggest risks facing not just them, but the whole corporate machine that they underwrite. Through working with key strategic sectors such as the insurance industry, the green movement has been able to carry its arguments to new audiences. The development of global markets in carbon, in the wake of international agreements on carbon trading to help reduce CO_2 emissions, is another example of a targeted effort to introduce green principles in a way that will have a system-wide effect. But governments around the world continue to be obsessed with short-term measures of economic competitiveness, while their inaction is a critical obstacle to progress towards the greens' goals.

Governments won't act alone. They fear moving ahead of the international policy pack and disadvantaging industry at a time of intensifying competitiveness. They also fear that their publics won't back action to integrate economy and environment if it threatens lifestyles, incomes and choice. Can the green movement that did so much to get environmental issues noticed now create the conditions for urgent action?

Is the personal still political?

For most of the radical greens of the 1970s who shaped today's environmentalist institutions the personal was political. There were no tidy demarcations between the conduct of private life and political convictions. The attitudes struck regarding local or global environmental issues were expected to be reflected in how you sourced your food and what you ate, your clothes, your house and how you travelled.

Does being green politically still demand that you are green *privately*? As with so much in green politics, the issue of climate change has magnified the consequences of their answers and actions. The great majority of greens, from reformists to radicals, believe that it is inconsistent to argue for, for example, significant reductions in CO_2 emissions at the level of the nation state, company or region without demonstrating some commitment to this goal at a personal level. But what this means in practical terms varies widely.

Some radicals eschew private cars and flying, and invest in installing their own renewable energy capacity and simplifying their lifestyles. Some have formed new communities – eco-villages – that are experimenting with what they see as the vanguard of new ways of living for all of us. At the more gradualist or reformist end of the spectrum greens have argued that they shouldn't have to step out of 'ordinary life' but rather look to demonstrate that we can all live well while reducing environmental impacts. Their solution to car driving or air travel might be to indulge in buying 'carbon offsets' (i.e. investing in, for example, tree planting that will balance their carbon emissions). Similarly, in countries where it is possible, these reformists are likely to look for chances to switch to a renewable electricity supplier, and purchase 'greener' appliances.

The radicals believe they are signalling the brutal reality of the changes society needs to follow if we are to achieve a sustainable society. The reformists believe they have found a route that most people can accept towards a less ecologically damaging way of life. Are these differences of philosophy and belief, or of tone and emphasis? Are they incompatible? The answer to that question might count for a good deal in the years to come as environmental politics moves centre stage. My own feeling is that personal lifestyle choices are constrained by a whole range of factors – family, work, social circle and more. Greens who can choose a low-impact lifestyle – often set apart from society – are enjoying a luxury that few in the green movement can afford.

I think it's a mistake – both philosophically and strategically – to insist on a particular model of green living. Indeed the most effective strategic move might now be to widen even further the spectrum of what it is to be green. Let anyone that makes even the most modest decision that favours the environment identify themselves as part of the green movement. Rather than setting the borders around itself according to a 'greener than thou' test of lifestyle commitment, greens need to see the enormous opportunities that lie in the widespread trend towards modest acts of care towards the environment. Greens must now work to reveal just how these acts connect to much bigger and longer term concerns. Individual changes and choices are important in signalling willingness for change, in pump-priming new products, technologies and services, and in helping people feel that their philosophy and lifestyle fit together in a manageable way. Many people who don't consider themselves greens as such are now concerned about the environment, and show it in small ways. Although these modest contributions won't result in solutions to the enormous challenges the green movement has done so much to identify, they do hint at enormous potential for political change that the green movement has yet to mobilize. To do that the green movement will need to change the case it puts to the world.

4

Conclusion
Turning green

It is thirty years since we started this work. Activities that dev-astate the environment and societies continue unabated. Today we are faced with a challenge that calls for a shift in our think-ing, so that humanity stops threatening its life-support system. We are called to assist the Earth to heal her wounds and in the process heal our own – indeed, to embrace the whole creation in all its diversity, beauty and wonder. This will happen if we see the need to revive our sense of belonging to a larger family of life, with which we have shared our evolutionary process. In the course of history, there comes a time when humanity is called to shift to a new level of consciousness, to reach a higher moral ground. A time when we have to shed our fear and give hope to each other. That time is now.[33]

The greens have achieved an extraordinary amount in the last three decades. But as Wangari Maathai's Nobel Prize acceptance speech above suggests, they have not reversed devastating trends that threaten life on earth. It is a robust cliché that the victors write history. Switch on the TV or open a newspaper and it seems as though the world runs on a motor of economic globalization and increasing consumption, with people every-where working harder to earn more. It can sometimes feel as though the neo-liberal victors of the twentieth century have already written not just our history but also the story of our future. But in the last thirty years greens have won increasingly influential support for their central insight: that the fortunes of the economy and society are ecologically rooted.

The green movement has been incubating some of the most powerful philosophical and political ideas of our age. They are powerful because they acknowledge that our lives have an eco-logical basis and call for a reordering of what we think of as the boundaries of ethical and political thinking. Greens promote radical thinking about time (both personal and planetary), values (both monetary and ethical) and interconnectedness. They offer the world an alternative to the systematic waste, suffering and hazard that goes with 'business as usual'. Slavery abolitionists of the eighteenth century and socialists and social democrats of the nineteenth and early twentieth centuries trans-formed the way capitalism worked. Greens could bring about another dramatic transformation and permanently change the terms of debate about progress.

But greens have sometimes made some of the most impor-tant new thinking of our era difficult to listen to. The movement was born out of threats to security and survival, and anxiety about loss of valued species and places. Greens have been nourished throughout by intermittent interest from the media. The various wings of the movement have fed the media with shrill predictions of ecological and social catastrophe – whether local or global. In early 2006 James Lovelock re-entered the debate with a popular science book in which he points to imminent catastrophe in more urgent terms than ever before. He suggests that our failure to address climate change means that 'our future is like that of the passengers on a small pleasure boat sailing quietly above the Niagara Falls, not knowing that the engines are about to fail.' [34] He goes on to suggest that 'the few breeding pairs of people that survive will be in the Arctic where the climate remains tolerable'.[35]

Lovelock's intention is at least in part to provoke urgent action. And greens have been true to form in promoting the catastrophism of this eminent scientist (even if most of them have been frustrated by his strong endorsement of nuclear power). In this, as in so many instances before, they bind together fearfulness and risk-aversion with calls for restraint and abstinence. It can seem that to follow the greens is to give up many of the pleasures of modern living. Greens often offer a frightening diagnosis of the future; yet insist on an unpalatable cure in the present. Can their arguments win meaningful support in wealthy democratic societies where people have plenty more immediate worries?

Green thinking has entered the language of everyday politics. But the job of making green ideas count is no less complex for that. The greens are threatened by the fact that, at a superficial level at least, we're all green now. Since the early 1990s most developed-world presidents, prime ministers and oil company chiefs have borrowed environmentalist rhetoric. The most recent – perhaps most surprising – example came in early 2006 with President Bush's acknowledgement that the USA needed to break its addiction to oil. In the same period Britain's new Conservative leader David Cameron emphasized new-formed green credentials as a component of the rejuvenation of his party.

The vocabulary of environmentalism has become increasingly evident in society and politics. But this leaves the movement with an enormous challenge: now that powerful figures have learned some green vocabulary, how can their words be turned into deeds? The difficulty of this was made clear when the British prime minister Tony Blair, who had previously claimed international leadership on climate change, told an international meeting of environment ministers that '(t)he blunt truth about the politics of climate change is that no country will want to sacrifice its economy in order to meet this challenge'.[36] How should greens react to this kind of pessimism/realism from senior politicians? How is widespread social awareness about ecological threats to be translated into radically new ways of designing things, doing business, taxing, trading, living?

The greens' dilemma has often been phrased as a choice between reformism and radicalism. On the one hand it is suggested that greens should look for gradual progress, for example through partnerships with sympathetic sections of government and business, to ratchet up environmental commitments. The radical position is to shift public opinion further away from existing models of economic development and set it on a course to an ecologically founded society.

This debate between reformism and radicalism is unproductive. Greens have long sustained a broad movement, embracing radical visionaries and short-term dealmakers. Many people who are advancing green thinking would not necessarily identify themselves as part of a movement. The green movement needs to sustain its breadth. Although it has created fierce debate and falling-out, this diversity has given the movement enormous flexibility during a period of rapid social, economic and technological change. Greens don't have to choose between long games and quick wins, between revolution or reform. But both of these forms of green politics need to adjust to fast-changing circumstances.

At first sight it might be said that the chances of taming some of the powerful forces of economic globalization, and redirecting the energies and capacities of human society, are slim. But the greens have an untapped potential to have a much deeper impact on contemporary politics and culture. Technological and cultural aspects of globalization are changing the potential practice and reach of environmental politics. This allows the creation of new global networks of surveillance and action. The capacity to move fluidly from global to local issues, and to call on 'witnesses' of environmental and social harm from across the world is a powerful tool. The green movement has not yet learnt how to use it fully.

The fast-paced technological and economic change that is part of globalization is usually portrayed by greens as a threat. But globalization also brings enormous opportunities to make rapid progress towards ecologically sustainable societies. In this context of change they need to reflect hard upon their role in the politics of risk and precaution, as they have both fed and fed off changing social attitudes to risk in contemporary society. There is now a danger that they will, inadvertently, promote static and unimaginative responses to ecological problems. Greens can and should be part of reviving excitement at the capacity for science, design and technology to transform lives. But this requires that greens explain their opposition to technologies such as GM or nuclear power more clearly.

Greens must lay more emphasis on the way decisions about science and technology are made, and how the benefits are distributed. They need to stop demonizing specific areas of life science and technology research without explanation. They also need to be ready to point to ecologically damaging consequences of policies that are born of green goals (biofuels and carbon offset policies hold such hazards).

Alongside this, green politics will also need to go beyond its stereotype and discover a sense of discovery, exuberance and optimism. In addition to being sharp eyed commentators on mainstream politics and business, greens need to make sure that their call to reduce ecological footprints is balanced with a politics that can offer pleasure and personal fulfilment at the individual level. Their origins and experience have left them remote from some of the most dynamic currents in contemporary culture. Greens should point to how we can reward ourselves with riches of time and opportunity. They should make sure that their arguments for reduced taxes on 'goods' such as work are heard as loudly as their demands for increased taxation of pollution 'bads'. By connecting people's thinking about environment, work and opportunity across the globe greens can argue for 'the good life' – in every sense – as the core of a positive politics of the future.

The green movement has made the world stop and think, but has not yet changed the way it works. It has achieved a great deal in reframing the way many of us think about our relationship with the natural world. Greens now need to move from diagnosing symptoms to offering a palatable cure. To do this they must make clear their own vision of the future. Many in the rich world suffer time-poverty, stress-related illness and index-linked unhappiness. At the same time the world's poorest face malnutrition, disease and illiteracy. If greens want to gather a majority around a radically revised version of how economies work they need to offer a vision that has human needs and interests centre stage. This is not to ignore or dismiss the ecologically based philosophy of Lovelock and Mary Midgley, or to propose a narrow humanism. Rather it is about carrying their insights into the everyday conversations and decisions through which both the richest and poorest people on the planet pursue security and happiness.

Greens have done a good job of communicating the perilous

state of the planet. But if they want to change the world for the better, they must reassess and refresh their capacity for flexibility and reinvention. The movement that is currently associated with delivering bad news must start to tell a story of how it is possible for people to lead a happier, more secure life, now and in the future. After decades as doom-mongers greens need to show that bringing ecology into politics can be very good news.

Notes

1 Note that in referring to a specific Green Party the word green will be capitalized – otherwise it will appear in lower case.

2 P. Henderson, *The Letters of William Morris to His Family and Friends* (New York: AMS Press, 1978 from the edition of 1950), p. 61.

3 R. Somervell, *A Protest against the Extension of Railways in the Lake District* (Windermere: J. Garnett, 1877), pp. 22–3.

4 W. Morris, *News from Nowhere: or, An Epoch of Unrest, Being Some Chapters from a Utopian Romance* in *The Collected Works of William Morris, Volume XVI* (London: Longmans, Green, 1992, first published 1890), pp. 3–211.

5 W. Morris, *How I Became a Socialist* in ibid. (London: Longmans, Green, 1992, first published 1894), pp. 279–80.

6 By 1860 the Great Crested Grebe was threatened by a fashion for dressing women's hats with their breeding plumage. The campaign both to change this practice and to establish safe reserves for birds demonstrated the benefits of working with the grain of the establishment.

7 H. D. Thoreau, *Walden or, Life in the Woods* (New York: Signet, 1960, first published 1854), p. 7.

8 Ibid., p. 66.

9 U. Thant, *Earth Day Proclamation*, 21 March 1971, www.themesh.com/un.html, accessed by author on 15/10/05.

10 M. Gandhi, *Collected Works of Mahatma Gandhi, Volume LXIV* (New Delhi: Publications Division, 1976), p. 217 quoted in Guha – see Further Reading.

11 Mendes had been campaigning to protect the Amazon rainfor-

est, native Brazilians and their fellow workers by defying loggers and cattle ranchers.

12   E. F. Schumacher, *Small Is Beautiful: A Study of Economics as if People Mattered* (London: Blond and Briggs, 1973), pp. 10–11.

13   Ibid., p. 143.

14   W. Rüdig, 'Between ecotopia and disillusionment: Green Parties in European government', in *Environment*, April, 2002, at www.globalgreens.info/literature/rudig/ecotopia.html, accessed by author on 9/11/05.

15   A. Naess, 'Sustainable development and the deep ecology movement', in S. Baker et al., eds., *The Politics of Sustainable Development* (Routledge, 1997), p. 64.

16   Ibid., p. 65.

17   V. Plumwood, *Feminism and the Mastery of Nature* (London: Routledge, 1993), p. 8.

18   V. Plumwood, *Environmental Culture: The Ecological Crisis of Reason* (London: Routledge, 2002), p. 235.

19   J. Lovelock, *Gaia: A New Look at Life on Earth* (Oxford: Oxford University Press, 1979), p. 9.

20   There are precedents: in the 1920s a Soviet scientist suggested a similar framework, but Lovelock and Margulis developed Gaia theory quite independently. See J. D. Oldfield and D. J. B. Shaw (2005), 'V. I. Vernadsky and the noosphere concept: Russian understandings of society–nature interaction' in *Geoforum*, available online 2 August 2005.

21   M. Midgley, *Gaia: The Next Big Idea* (London: Demos, 2001), p. 11.

22   IPCC, Third Assessment Report, 2001 Summary for Policymakers, www.ipcc.ch/pub/spm22–01.pdf, accessed by author on 3/12/05, p. 8.

23   www.climatehotmap.org/index.html, accessed by author on 17/11/05.

24   www.climatehotmap.org/africa.html, accessed by author on 29/11/05.

25   It is important to note that James Lovelock has frustrated many in the green movement with his vocal support for nuclear energy as part of society's response to climate change. His latest book sees

nuclear power as central to a 'controlled descent' from a carbon based economy.

26 www.sehn.org/wing.html, accessed by author on 14/10/05.

27 E. von Weizsacker, et al., *Factor Four: Doubling Wealth, Halving Resource Use – A report to the Club of Rome* (London: Earthscan, 1998).

28 R. John McNeill, *Something New under the Sun: An Environmental History of the Twentieth Century* (London: Penguin, 2000), p. 336.

29 H. E. Daly, *Ecological Economics: The Concept of Scale and its Relation to Allocation, Distribution, and Uneconomic Growth* (for CANSEE, 16–19 October 2003, Jasper, Alberta, Canada, www.cansee.org/cdocs/2003HDaly.pdf, accessed by author on 3/12/05), p. 12.

30 J. Proops, 'Ecological economics: rationale and problem areas', in *Ecological Economics* 1(1): 59–76, 1989, pp. 73–4.

31 R. Costanza, 'What is ecological economics?' in *Ecological Economics* 1(1): 1–7, 1989, p. 5.

32 J. Loh and M. Wackernagel, (2004), *Living Planet Report 2004*, WWF International, Gland, Switzerland.

33 Wangari Maathai (2004), Nobel Peace Prize Acceptance Speech, Oslo, Norway, www.glomna.org/a.php?id=34, accessed by author on 9/11/05.

34 James Lovelock, *The Revenge of Gaia* (London: Allen Lane, 2006), p. 6.

35 James Lovelock, 'The Earth is about to catch a morbid fever that may last as long as 100,000 years', *Independent*, 19 February 2006.

36 Tony Blair, Climate Change Speech, 1 November 2005, accessed by author at www.number10.gov.uk/output/Page8437.asp on 22/2/06.

Glossary

acid rain/acid deposition: sulphur oxides from industrial sources such as coal-fired power stations or metal smelters which can be transported over long distances and affect ecosystems hundreds of miles away.

biodiversity: short for 'biological diversity', refers to the variability amongst living organisms, including within species, between species, and of ecosystems. Has become a shorthand for describing threatened species and habitats.

CFCs/chlorofluorocarbons: identified in the mid-1980s as the family of industrially produced chemicals responsible for causing the ozone hole (*see* below).

climate change/global warming: the accelerating effect on the naturally occurring greenhouse effect (*see* below) which climate scientists attribute to the enormous quantities of carbon dioxide that human societies have released into the atmosphere since the Industrial Revolution (and in particular, since the Second World War) with hazardous consequences for both humans and the natural world.

conservation: threats from human development to species and habitats became understood from the late nineteenth century onwards, energizing new branches of scientific study and lobby groups that are now major institutions (e.g. RSPB). The term 'biodiversity' (*see* above) is often used synonymously.

deep ecology: coined by Norwegian, Arne Naess, this philosophical approach has been particularly influential in North America. It starts from a 'vivid expression of deep concern for non-humans' and represents a shift in the centre of gravity of political concern towards the non-human world.

desertification: the degradation of land in arid, semi arid and dry regions as a result of various factors including climatic variations and human activities including agriculture.

eco-fascism: a critique of authoritarian greens who, it is charged, would ignore democratic or liberal traditions and institutions in the interests of the environment.

eco-feminism: a combination of green and feminist thought that explains men's domination of women and men's domination over nature as related problems.

ecological economics: a radical branch of environmental economics that goes further in integrating ecological values and limits. It promotes wider public participation in decision-making and experimental approaches to expressing environmental interests in decisions.

ecological/environmental footprint: A tool for calculating the environmental impact of an individual, a city, a country or human society as a whole. Partly developed as a communications tool to try to bring wider understanding of the consequences of different choices.

ecological/green taxation: greens argue for a shift away from the taxation of 'goods' such as work through e.g. income tax and employer contributions towards the taxation of 'bads', above all pollution. Proposed carbon taxes to respond to climate change are the most widely discussed form.

factor four: an argument put by green economists and technologists that resource productivity can – and should – grow fourfold. In other words the amount of wealth extracted from one unit of natural resource can quadruple. The argument is that people can live twice as well – yet use half the natural resources.

gaia hypothesis: also known as earth systems science, a theory developed mainly by James Lovelock that defined the earth – Gaia – as a complex entity made up of multiple feedbacks between biosphere, atmosphere, oceans and soil, amounting to a system that seeks 'an optimum physical and chemical environment for life on this planet'.

global warming: *see* climate change

globalization: summarizes changes brought about by greatly increased international trade in the last decades of the twentieth century. The term can refer to economic, political or cultural globalization, although these are inextricably interlinked.

greenhouse effect: the naturally occurring process by which the atmosphere maintains a higher temperature on earth than would otherwise be the case. It is the increased quantities of so-called greenhouse gases (such as carbon dioxide) that is causing the enhanced greenhouse effect, or climate change (*see* above).

Green Parties: the usual title taken where the green movement has spawned political parties that contest democratic elections in order to further ecological goals.

IPCC (Intergovernmental Panel on Climate Change): the global scientific review process designed to summarize the state of current knowledge about climate change (by the process of anonymous checking and reviewing of research known as peer review). The IPCC provides summaries of the science for the international policy-making community.

Kyoto Protocol: the international agreement reached in 1997 in Japan and ratified (came into force) in 2004 when enough countries agreed to abide by it. It includes targets and timetables for reducing the main greenhouse gases in developed economies, though some countries, including the USA, have refused to ratify.

Montreal Protocol: the 1987 international agreement to phase out use of CFCs (*see* above) that was agreed with surprising speed to respond to the scientific evidence about ozone depletion (*see* below).

ozone hole/depletion: CFCs (*see* above) that had been widely used in refrigeration, cleaning and packaging products, and as gas propellants since the 1950s, were implicated in the destruction of a layer of gas that protected the earth from harmful levels of ultraviolet radiation.

Romanticism/the Romantic movement: a movement in the arts and literature that arose in part in response to the threats generated by the rapid industrialization of the nineteenth century. They viewed nature as a source of beauty, spiritual renewal and fulfilment.

social ecology: associated with the American Murray Bookchin, it is a variant of green political philosophy that blends ecological and anarchist insights.

soil erosion: the displacement of soil by the action of, for example, wind and water over time. Although it is a natural process it can be increased by poor land use practices such as deforestation, overgrazing and the construction of roads or tracks.

sustainability: *see* sustainable development

sustainable development: a proposal for a form of capitalist economic development that integrates economic, social and environmental interests that many greens dismiss as empty rhetoric. The classic 'Brundtland definition' is of 'a form of sustainable development which meets the needs of the present without compromising the ability of future generations to meet their own needs'.

UNCED: the United Nations Conference on Environment and Development in 1992, also known as the Earth Summit, was the largest meeting of world leaders to date and brought the concept of sustainable development onto the international stage.

Timeline

1661 John Evelyn writes 'Fumifugium, or, The Inconveniencie of the Aer and Smoak of London Dissipated' to propose remedies for London's air pollution problem. These include large public parks and lots of flowers. He also proposes measures to reverse deforestation caused by the rapid expansion of ship-building to supply the navy.

1836 Ralph Waldo Emerson writes *Nature* and founds the Transcendentalist movement.

1854 H. D. Thoreau publishes his account of living in nature, *Walden*, strongly influenced by Emerson.

1889 American writer and naturalist John Muir begins the campaign to save the Yosemite region in California from exploitation. His articles in *Century Magazine* sparked a bill in Congress to expand federal protection. This work results in the creation of the first National Parks.

1926 Russian scientist Vladimir Vernadsky publishes his theories concerning the integration of the biosphere, or living matter, and the earth's geological processes.

1956 The deaths of one thousand Londoners are blamed on a killer smog (a mixture of smoke and fog), forcing the British Parliament to pass the Clean Air Act.

1956 Mysterious illnesses among the population of the small town of Minamata in Japan are found to be caused by mercury poisoning resulting from industrial pollution. Business and government attempts at a cover-up create the world's first environmental scandal, attracting worldwide media interest.

1957 The International Geophysical Year helps to establish a global scientific community concerned with exploring planetary processes.

This lays the ground for the studies that point to human-induced climate change.

1962 American science writer Rachel Carson enters the best-seller lists with *Silent Spring*. This account of the impact of industrial agricultural chemicals on wildlife sets the tone for more systematic critiques of the consequences of unfettered economic development.

1967 The hull of the *Torrey Canyon* oil tanker breaks open off the picturesque south coast of England, creating a huge media event.

1969 Friends of the Earth founded in the USA.

1971 Greenpeace founded in Canada.

1972 The United Nations Conference on the Human Environment meets in Stockholm, Sweden, and the UN Environment Programme (UNEP) is formed to implement the recommendations of the Stockholm meeting.

1972 The *Limits to Growth* report is published. Drafted by a panel of experts, and published by the Club of Rome, it lends authority to the environmentalist case.

1973 A world 'oil crisis' sparked by an increasingly powerful body of oil-producing nations, illustrates environmentalist claims about energy scarcity.

1973 E. F. Schumacher publishes *Small Is Beautiful: A Study of Economics as if People Mattered*. Schumacher's ideas give shape to emergent ideas about how a green economy might work.

1977 World Environment Day marks the beginning of Kenya's Green Belt Movement, founded by Wangari Maathai. By 1992 the Green Belt Movement has planted over seven million saplings, proving the effectiveness of grassroots organization and 'appropriate technology'.

1979 Three Mile Island nuclear power plant partially melts down when cooling systems fail: a major blow to an industry that had already suffered a catalogue of other problems including massive cost overruns, waste dumping and technical failures.

1979 Radical direct action group Earth First! is established by Arizona desert activists Dave Foreman, Howie Wolke and Mike Roselle.

1979 James Lovelock publishes *Gaia: A New Look at Life on Earth*. Lovelock theorizes that the earth is a self-regulating entity maintaining optimal conditions for life.

1980 *The World Conservation Strategy* is published and becomes a basis for many national conservation plans in developing nations.

1984 Bhopal disaster in India caused by Union Carbide's fertilizer plant. The plant leaks methyl isocyanate in Indian town of Bhopal. Estimates suggest 2,000 die, with another 8,000 dying later of chronic effects and a further 100,000 injured. Environmental NGOs ensure that the disaster keeps wider issues of industrial pollution and corporate responsibility in the headlines around the world for years to come.

1986 In the USSR, nuclear reactor number 4 explodes at Chernobyl causing around 4,200 deaths to date, another major blow to public confidence in the nuclear industry.

1985 An 'ozone hole' above Antarctica is discovered by British scientists, and is explained in terms of release of CFCs by industry and consumer products.

1987 The Montreal Protocol international agreement to phase out ozone-depleting chemicals is signed by 24 countries, including the USA, Japan, Canada and the EEC nations, demonstrating that fast and effective action on a global environmental issue was possible.

1988 Assassination by ranchers of Chico Mendes, leader of Brazil's rubber tappers' union Chiapas, and a prominent figure in the movement to save the rainforest from illegal loggers and ranchers. Mendes's death was one of 1,700 resulting from land disputes in Brazil over two decades.

1990 The United Nations Intergovernmental Panel on Climate Change (IPCC), the biggest international peer-review process in history, produces its First Assessment Report.

1991 Nigeria's Movement for the Survival of the Ogoni People is founded by Ken Saro-Wiwa in reaction to Shell's oil drilling and extensive pollution in the Niger river delta. The country's military dictators responded to massive demonstrations with threats, intimidation, arrest of the leaders and, in 1995, their execution. Shell becomes the target of global campaigns concerning social and environmental responsibility. Ken Saro-Wiwa becomes an environmentalist icon.

1992 The UN Earth Summit is held in Rio de Janiero, Brazil. The conference drafts a vision for sustainable development – *Agenda 21* – as well as conventions on climate change and biodiversity.

1995 Shell and Greenpeace battle over the disposal of the Brent Spar North Sea oil storage platform. Shell are forced to change their plans but Greenpeace suffers its own PR disaster when it admits to making mistakes in the presentation of pollution risks.

1997 The Kyoto Protocol is adopted by 122 nations. It sets out targets, timetables and mechanisms for carbon dioxide (CO_2) reductions. Environmentalists criticize it as 'too little too late'. Politicians from the USA and Australia argue that meeting Kyoto obligations threatens their countries' way of life.

1999 The UN estimates that the human population of planet earth exceeds six billion, with more than half living in cities.

2001 US President George Bush reverses environmentalist measures linked to pollution and wildlife protection. In the same year street protests at the G8 meeting in Genoa, Italy, attract worldwide media attention.

2002 The German government, formed out of a coalition of the SDP and the Green Party, announces plans for a massive increase in wind generation capacity over the next 25 years.

2002 The UN's World Summit on Sustainable Development, ten years on from Rio's Earth Summit, is felt by the green movement to be muted and frustrating. Environmentalist leaders charge big business and governments with doing no more than learning green rhetoric.

2004 Wangari Maathai, Kenyan Environment Minister and grassroots activist, becomes the first African woman to be awarded the Nobel Peace Prize.

2005 The Kyoto Protocol, which structures international agreement on climate change, comes into force after Russia ratifies it in late 2004.

Further Reading

Environmental and green politics and theory are now well served by a thoughtful and critical body of work. The following titles are particularly helpful:

Carter, Neil, *The Politics of the Environment: Ideas, Activism, Policy*, (Cambridge: Cambridge University Press, 2001)
A thorough and approachable textbook that has a wide scope on the politics of the environment

Daly, Herman and Cobb, John B. Jr, *For the Common Good: Redirecting the Economy toward Community, the Environment, and a Sustainable Future* (Boston: Beacon Press Books, 1994)
A clear statement of the argument for an ecologically informed economics

Dobson, Andrew, 'Ecological citizenship' in *Debating the Earth* (Oxford: Oxford University Press, 2004)
Argues for a new ecological basis to thinking about citizenship as a powerful foundation for a green society

Doherty, Brian, *Ideas and Actions in the Green Movement* (London: Routledge, 2002)
Takes on the difficult task of trying to pin down green political ideology

Eckersley, Robyn, *The Green State: Rethinking Democracy and Sovereignty* (Cambridge, Ms: MIT Press, 2004)
Binds together green political theory and current debates about the state and democracy to try to give a sense of what a 'green state' might look like.

Guha, Ramachandra, *Environmentalism: A Global History* (Reading: Longman, 2000)
A short and readable summary of environmentalism's history that is particularly valuable for widening the scope of the study beyond Europe and North America

Plumwood, Val, *Environmental Culture: The Ecological Crisis of Reason* (London: Routledge, 2002)
A feminist philosopher finds the dominant Western models of reason to be at the root of ecological problems

Woodin, Mike and Lucas, Caroline, *Green Alternatives to Globalisation* (London: Pluto Press, 2004)
Written by two longstanding Green Party activists from the UK, this puts the case for green policies targeted at the negative environmental and social consequences of economic globalization.

Useful websites and contacts

Green issues and the web grew up together, with the result that the Internet is a very rich resource of information and opinion. I haven't included websites or contact details for the main environmental groups, as they are easily found via the Internet or a phonebook. Much of the information available on the Internet needs to be handled with care, but the following sites are very good starting points for finding out more about the green movement or specific environmental issues:

• BBC: There are some excellent Internet news providers on environmental issues, but the BBC's one (especially its science and nature section) offers well-written and carefully balanced reporting: www.bbc.co.uk

• green parties: green parties around the world have websites of widely varying content. Here is a portal that will help you find contact details and policy information from a particular green party, or to track some of the networking activity: www.greens.org/

• Oneworld.net: this global network is a very rich resource for news and contact details on the environment, development and human rights: www.oneworld.net/

• openDemocracy: Their debate on climate change is a nice blend of political and scientific debate, written in an approachable style. There are other environment-related materials on the site: www.opendemocracy.net/climate_change/

• Planet Ark: the core of this site is the Reuters news agencies' environment stories of the day from around the world. More international than the BBC site, and also with more links to actions you can take: www.planetark.org/

• United Nations Environment Programme: UNEP is a good first stop for materials on the state of international knowledge and action on a range of issues, including biodiversity loss, climate change, deforestation, pollution and more, tailored to different audience needs. There are links to the work of more narrowly focused international bodies: www.unep.org/

Index

Also in the series and available from Granta Books
www.granta.com

WHAT DO BUDDHISTS BELIEVE?

Tony Morris

'*I believe that every human being has an innate desire for happiness and does not want to suffer. I also believe that the very purpose of life is to experience this happiness.*' The Dalai Lama

Buddhism is one of the world's oldest and most widespread belief-systems. Virtually unknown outside Asia until the last century, it is now the fastest growing religion in the West and has nearly half a billion adherents throughout the world. What is it about Buddhism that attracts so many in an age when people seem to be turning away from organized religion?

The teachings of Buddhism are many and varied, and it has a well-developed philosophical and mystical dimension; but at its core is a simple set of propositions and practices designed to meet the practical day-to-day concerns of ordinary people: how to live a compassionate, creative, wise and, above all, happy life.

WHAT DO CHRISTIANS BELIEVE?

Malcolm Guite

'*I give you a new commandment, that you love one another.
Just as I have loved you, you also should love one another.*'
Jesus Christ

Christianity grew from a minor sect within Judaism to become
one of the major world religions. What started as a small group
of people from a common background is now a movement
which embraces many different languages and cultures, giving
rise to an astonishing variety of practices and interpretations.

Yet all Christians have a common basis of shared faith inspired
by the life and teaching of a carpenter from Nazareth. How has
this happened? Malcolm Guite's book shows how Jesus himself
identified love as the essential element in both worship and
daily life.

WHAT DO MUSLIMS BELIEVE?

Ziauddin Sardar

'*The world is green and beautiful; and God has appointed you as His trustee over it*' Prophet Muhammad

Islam is one of the great monotheistic religions of the world. Its teachings emphasize unity, humility, forgiveness and love of God. The Qur'an sings the virtues of knowledge and rationality. The life of Muhammad demonstrates the importance of tolerance, social justice and brotherhood. In Sufism, Islam presents a mystical system based on love and devotion. So, why is Islam often associated with hatred, violence, obstinacy and bigotry?

Ziauddin Sardar examines the true teachings of Islam and explores the reality of the Muslim world today. Emphasizing the diversity of Islam and its ideals, he assesses the role Islam plays in the lives of ordinary Muslims and shows how Islamic beliefs and practices help Muslims understand the modern world.

WHAT DO DRUIDS BELIEVE?

Philip Carr-Gomm

'*Above all else, Druidry means following a spiritual path rooted in the green Earth.*' John Michael Greer

Druidism evolved out of the tribal cultures of Britain, Ireland and western France over two thousand years ago. In the seventeenth century it experienced a revival which has continued to this day.

Druidry's modern worldwide appeal lies in its focus on reverence for the natural world, a belief in the value of personal creativity, and of developing a sense of communion with the powers of nature and the spirit. Its startling recent growth derives from its broad appeal: some treat it as a philosophy, others as a religion, still others as a path of self-development. Philip Carr-Gomm explains the practical value of following Druidism today, and examines its core beliefs and relevance to the contemporary issues that face us all.

WHAT DO EXISTENTIALISTS BELIEVE?

Richard Appignanesi

'*Necessity makes existentialists of us all . . . It is a map drawn truthfully to our likeness.*'

Existentialism is not a unified doctrine in any conventional sense. It breaks ranks with all previous philosophy, unsettles orthodox religion, and questions the supremacy of science. However, the question it poses is of fundamental importance to us all: what on earth am I to make of my existence?

In this lively and provocative new introduction to existentialism, Richard Appignanesi challenges the reader to take part in a series of 'thought experiments' in order to illuminate what it means to approach the question of our being human existentially. He also traces the development of existential thought through the writings of its founding thinkers such as Søren Kierkegaard, Friedrich Nietzsche, Edmund Husserl, Martin Heidegger and Jean-Paul Sartre and looks at existentialism's encounters with Islam, Freud, feminism, race and the notion of progress.

WHAT DO ASTROLOGERS BELIEVE

Nicholas Campion

'And God said, "Let there be lights in the firmament of the heavens to separate the day from the night; and let them be for signs and for seasons and for days and years."' *Genesis I.14*

Astrology, the notion that the stars and planets hold significance for human life, exists in most cultures. It is evident in Stone Age lunar calendars dating back to 30,000 BCE. Today, ninety per cent of Indians consult astrologers about their forthcoming marriages while over fifty per cent of people in the West read their horoscopes in newspapers or magazines.

How has this pre-Christian, pre-scientific view of the cosmos survived to the present day and what is its enduring appeal?

Astrology's techniques and philosophical foundations are complex and there is no single tradition. Here Nicholas Campion explores astrology's past and present, its claims and appeal, and explains what astrologers really believe.

WHAT DO JEWS BELIEVE

Edward Kessler

There is a story about a Jew who travels from Israel to the United States. When he returns, he tells his friend some of the amazing things he has seen. 'I met a Jew who had grown up in a yeshiva and knew large sections of the Talmud by heart. I met a Jew who was an atheist. I met a Jew who owned a large business and I met a Jew who was an ardent communist.' 'So what's so strange?' the friend asks. 'America is a big country and millions of Jews live there.' 'You don't understand,' the man answers, 'it was the same Jew.'

Judaism is not simply a series of beliefs. It is a practice and a way of life. *What do Jews Believe?* explores the variety of ways Jews live their lives: religious and secular, Ashkenazi and Sephardi, Jews in Israel and Jews who live in the diaspora. It asks what Judaism is and what it means to be a Jew.